FAKE PAPERS

Survival Lessons from Grandma's Escape

BY AARON ROCKETT

**AARON ROCKETT
BOOKS**

www.aaronrockett.com

Library of Congress-in-Publication Data

Rockett, Aaron.
Fake Papers: Survival Lessons from Grandma's Escape
/ Aaron Rockett
p.   cm.

ISBN: 978-1-7329741-0-4 pbk.

AARON ROCKETT BOOKS
www.aaronrockett.com

For Beth and Rory
With love

Contents

Acknowledgement

I want to convey my heartfelt appreciation for the many people who steered me through this book. They offered me encouragement, read, discussed, provided feedback, and even proofread and edited. Most of all I want to thank my wife, Beth who was there through every step of the long, yet cathartic journey, and a big thank you to my parents, Edward Rockett and Lorin Grean, for your enthusiasm and support of the book.

My deepest gratitude goes to Tom Judge, who years before me, sat with my grandma and meticulously documented her story, writing it down so it would never disappear. Thank you to Roy Hoffman, whose insights about my first draft guided the rest of the work, and to Tom Leja for invaluable help with the cover design. I want to also thank Robert O. Paxton for aiding my research into Vichy France, and my aunt, Tina Bird, for all the family photos and documents.

Last, but certainly not least, I want to thank my baby daughter, Rory, who reminds me daily what is really important: Snacks, giggles, blueberry fingers and soft squeezes.

1

Find a spark of connectivity.

Panjshir Valley, Afghanistan

The guard, tugging at his beard, watched me and then turned his head to the cameraman trotting over Massoud's sacred grounds, a windswept stretch of rocks and beige dirt. Through the mausoleum's windows covered in a thin layer of dust my gaze shifted between the cameraman, John, his wispy, blonde hair blowing carelessly in the breeze and the guards, whose black eyes squinted in the blaring sun, Kalashnikov rifles at their sides.

Our translator, Jawad, a small, young man with a trimmed beard walked over to me. "We have problem," he said, pulling at my arm. "They call you, 'American, Jew, spy.' They hate you."

The guards stood next to a broken down bus that was their guard-house in the middle of the isolated mountain range. They wore green army jackets, one had a turban and the other a pakool— a flat, round, wool hat that was rolled tight at the bottom.

Ahmed Shah Massoud's concrete tomb commanded a holy place atop this hill where we filmed. He was a celebrated general who battered the Taliban before Osama Bin Laden had him assassinated. The attackers posed as a camera crew.

While John framed up shots and dusted off his lens, Jawad nodded at the broken down bus. "They hate you," he said again. I moved slowly in the direction of Massoud's men hearing the gravel crunch under my boots and put my hand up with a wave. In the corner of my eye I saw a teenage boy in a grey, wool sweater, whom I hadn't noticed earlier, step up from behind our yellow car and then disappear inside the bus.

"Tell them how much I respect Massoud," I said to Jawad. "We are here to honor him." Jawad started translating. Then there was only silence on the hill amidst lifeless grasses and peaks of sharp boulders, except for the distant skidding of John's boots over rocks.

The man in a turban wrapped around his head spat out a few words that rolled off his tongue like a soft gurgle.

"They invite you for tea," Jawad said. "You should have tea with them."

I followed them to padded bus benches around a fire pit outside the guardhouse where a charred kettle steamed on a grill. One guard poured a cup and handed it to me.

"What are their names?" I asked.

"Hassan," Jawed said. "And Akmal."

"My name is Aaron," I said tapping my chest with my hand. Their black eyes widened and Akmal's eyes were actually as green as my mother's.

"Awww, Harun," said Akmal under his breath and then spoke with resolute purpose.

"Harun is Muslim name in Quran," Jawad translated for me, and then studied my eyes. "He asks, 'are you Muslim?'"

I didn't expect the question. Until that moment I had paid little attention to my name or being a Jew. My grandma's story was just a hazy memory. Yet, it was grandma that once told me as a child that Harun and Aaron were both from the same Ancient Egyptian name, *aha rw*.

"Tell him," I paused, thinking about what grandma had said. "Tell him, I believe in the same God he does." Jawad translated. To this both guards smiled, nodded at me and sipped their tea. Jawad also smiled and for the first time the tension left his face. Minutes earlier I

2

was an "American, Jew, spy." Now I sipped the hot water tasting bits of floating tea and felt the warmness in my throat.

I wondered how these men would have reacted if I told them I was named for my grandma's father, Aron, an Orthodox Jew from a rural village in Poland. My family was Jewish, but I knew little of this heritage, having instead attended Catholic high school and college.

Our car's windows rattled down the steep, rocky road away from the tomb. I breathed out a sigh. About fifty yards down we dipped and our right side wobbled. The loud flapping noise was a flat tire. Jawad pulled a three-inch, rusty nail from the worn tread. We jacked the car up in the dirt and pulled our spare out and were back on the road in no time. About twenty feet later the other back tire wobbled and went flat. Another nail, same as the last. Our tires were spiked and I now knew what the teen was doing crouched behind our car.

As the tire was being rolled by hand along the rutted road to a village a mile away to be fixed (we didn't have another spare), a head with black hair peered over the side of a ravine. It was a man wearing a camouflage jacket and holding a rifle. He started walking on the road towards me and spoke into a walkie-talkie. I looked back to Massoud's tomb and at the guards now watching us through binoculars on the hill.

The man approached with the rifle pointed down. He had jet-black hair, bangs cut straight across his forehead, a thick beard, and a fierce scowl. He stood on the edge of the dirt road five feet from me looking down at John filming by the river and then back at me.

I only thought about grandma's story she once told me as a child. I pulled a digital camera out of my pocket, gesturing if he wanted his picture taken. He nodded.

When I showed him the picture he put his hand out and I shook his firm, rough grip. "Tashakor," he said, and slung his rifle on his shoulder and continued towards Massoud's tomb.

Standing in the crisp air I stared into the clear river of the Panjshir Valley seeing its powerful ripples cutting through the rocks, which

3

gave life to walnut and apple orchards. My grandma was a world away from here waiting to die and it was her life that somehow brought me to this place. I suddenly knew what I had to do.

2

Question wants.

Palo Alto, CA

I lived 3,000 miles away from grandma in Washington, DC, and I was her nearest relative. She relegated herself to a small corner of the globe, away from family, declining numerous invitations to live with my aunt in England. I thought grandma preferred to die alone and without anybody knowing the wiser. "I hurt all over, I'm ready to go," she told me every phone conversation. She was 90 and death wouldn't come soon enough. Her house was downsized to a small condo and then to a room in a convalescent home in close stride with her withering body, but her mind was still sharp.

"I've never met your girlfriend," she said. It was always the first inquiry when I visited every few years and it was no different this time. "It's okay if you don't have one."

"No, I don't."

"What's that?" She had trouble hearing me. "Don't you want to get married? Have children? I'm not getting any younger."

"One day, maybe."

"That's fine. No pressure. Just know, if you're gay, I'll love you just the same."

"Grandma, I'm not gay."

"Things are different these days. What do I know?"

Draped in a Mayan-patterned muumuu, she pushed herself up from the Barcalounger. Her small room was filled with smells of Europe and tapestries hung on the wall from Guatemala of women carrying baskets.

I remained quiet not answering her prodding. I had many questions of my own about my mom that I didn't ask her. I wondered if grandma still hated my father. Still blamed him. But I came for another purpose.

"I want to record your story," I finally said.

"I don't like to dredge up those memories," she said after a moment considering my question.

"You've told me before. When I was a kid."

"That was different."

"But this is different," I said.

She had a small piece of chocolate in her hand and a cup of tea as she took small steps back to her recliner. It was grandma's story that inspired me to meet the South African president, Nelson Mandela, which I used my student I.D. to gain access through the "Press Entrance" of the Parliament Buildings in Cape Town, and led to my career.

"Grandma, it's important to preserve your story."

She lifted her stare from the rug and I saw in her eyes she didn't want to, but I knew for me, she would.

She set her chocolate down on a nightstand and rustled through a closet, her small frame disappearing in the colorful frocks as she found a fur hat, and put on red lipstick. I set up a chair and staged nick-knacks from her travels as a backdrop. I pressed record on the camera. She lowered herself into the chair and held a tissue in her hands and dabbed the saliva that ran unimpeded from the corners of her lips through the creases of her chin like tributaries.

"I was young and stupid," she said, her steel, grey eyes that were once green, now just acquiescent. "I wanted the war to come. I hoped it was true that there was war."

3

Mind your signature.

Antwerp, Belgium

Small slivers of light shot through cracks in the windowless building. A bookkeeper sat in the front room under a lamp jotting numbers in a ledger. Aron Schmidt sat at his desk in an office that looked out over the warehouse and held up sweater samples comparing fabrics. His sweater business was growing in Antwerp just as Adolf Hitler was finding success in politics over the border in Germany.

Letty, my grandma, never saw her father's business, but her sister Annie rode the ferry over the Scheldt River to Sint Niklaas to visit him one day when she was thirteen. The boat took her through a thick mist to the industrial part of Antwerp.

"Come in my little *bubala*," father said waving her into his office surprised to see his daughter. For Annie, father was an escape from the harshness of mother. Annie just had her first menstruation and after telling mother, was smacked on the back of the head.

"Let me show you around," father said. He took her arm wrapping it close to his and didn't ask why his daughter showed up at the factory. "This is our production facility." He swung his arm out over the expanse filled with bundles of cloth. He held Annie's hand, but as they stepped towards the office door the bookkeeper burst in holding the ledger. He stabbed the paper with his finger.

"This can't be right," he said. "This can't be right."

Father looked at the paper he jabbed with his thumb. Annie saw confusion on father's face and then the color drain to an opaque yellow. He recited the numbers and his lips moved behind his beard as he read the statement. The look of puzzlement turned to fear.

"How?" he said to himself.

"Is everything alright, *Tatti*?" Annie said.

"Yes, *bubala*. *Tatti* needs to attend to this matter. I'll see you at home." Annie walked toward the door and looked back at father knowing something wasn't right.

Later, when he came through the door that night his eyes were strained and his smile forced. He put his hat on the rack and set his bag down. His vacant stare skimmed over the living room and the lamplight caught the furrows around his eyes.

"How are my *bubalas*?" He kneeled down hugging his three daughters. They were dressed like dolls wearing the exact same bobbed haircut, velvet dresses, and leather shoes. Letty, the youngest, dug her hands into his jacket pockets with her sisters, Annie and Suzy, searching for caramel treats. She found one under his handkerchief. He kissed them each on their foreheads and his eyes were clouded as he gazed at his girls unwrapping the caramel treats.

"You spoil them too much," Blima said. Their mother's arms were folded while she stood in the doorway between the kitchen and living room wearing a wig (customary for Hasidic Jews, although she was not) and imposing her shadow on the apartment. Father looked up at his wife, Blima, shamefaced as he indulged his daughters.

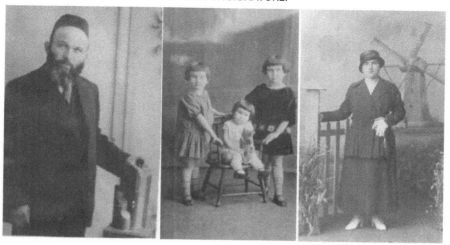

Father, Aron (left), the three sisters (Annie, left, Letty, center, Suzy, right), and mother, Blima (right).

"Our lives would be a lot better if my other marriage was allowed to happen," Blima told the girls. Father was always known for running from the law. He spent most of his life dodging authorities. A favorite of his tricks was to blur his paper trail by using different names, which he did on his daughters' birth certificates. On one occasion when he was young, he even jumped out a second story window of his sister's farmhouse to escape fighting in the Great War. He rolled up his sleeve with a mischievous grin to show his girls the scars from the fall.

Blima and Aron grew up in villages in Poland 14 miles apart. The first time they ever met was under the marriage-canopy with a matchmaker, about to exchange vows. The injustice of that marriage overwhelmed Blima so much that her bitterness clouded even the good things. Making the sting of marrying Aron worse, the "other" man Blima was supposed to marry made a huge fortune, a fact she never let Aron forget. The way she saw it, all she had in life now was Judaism and three daughters to keep "pure."

That night at dinner Aron announced he was leaving on a business trip to London. Annie wondered if it had to do with what had happened

9

at the warehouse, but Letty, 10 at the time, thought nothing of it and enjoyed the brisket mother cooked. She heard father moving through the rooms in the early chill before the sun rose gathering his things quietly so as not to wake the house. The front door opened and Letty felt a draft of cool air rush over her and she shivered. Then the door closed and her bed felt warm and cozy.

A letter came from father days later postmarked in England. Letty watched as mother opened it and her face turn red and her fingers clench the letter tight. It was a mixture of shock and fury.

"That fool!" she said. "He has destroyed this family!" Her lips tightened and she wiped her eyes with a dishtowel. Mother didn't say anything more, but her head looked as if it might pop. Letty didn't dare ask her what was wrong and waited for Suzy to come home. The only daughter Blima trusted was Suzy, who was the oldest. It was a long hour and Letty strained to hear the creaking floorboards of the apartment hallway announcing her sister, one of the only times she ever looked forward to her coming home.

When Suzy came through the door that afternoon mother unleashed a violent assault of Yiddish and Polish words. Letty heard it from the living room, crawling as close to the kitchen door as she dared resting her head on the wall. Her heart pounded in her chest, as she understood father was never coming back.

"It's shocking," a lawyer said as he looked over the paperwork with Blima and Annie, neither of whom knew why Aron's business failed. "Your husband's business partners embezzled all the funds from the company account. What makes matters worse, your husband is the only one to place his signature for the operating loans, so he is the one on the hook for the debt. Your father will go to debtor's prison for at least five years and you're now responsible for his debt."

Without consulting mother, father opted for exile in London over debtor's prison. He left Blima, who had never worked a day in her life, didn't speak the languages of Belgium (French or Flemish), nor had ever received an education beyond nine years old, to clean up the mess and hide valuables from creditors, and his daughters to figure out a way to make money.

4

Listen to the hairs on your neck.

It was her cousin, Hanka, who landed Letty her first job in the diamond market at 13. The job was with Alexander Behr, an English Jew who ran the Palestine and Orient Lloyd Agency in the Diamond Exchange. Letty ran deliveries and posted the arriving and departing ocean liners bound for New York, London and other international destinations.

Some said Mr. Behr chose his company name with the aim of snaring unwary customers looking for the Peninsular and Orient Agency, an already well-established business.

"You employ such fine looking ladies, Alexander," said one old patron looking Letty over, still only a girl with wavy, brown hair, big cheeks and small, soft lips. Her socks hung around her ankles, frayed with overuse.

"Chaim, let's examine your recent appraisals," Mr. Behr said steering the conversation back to business and then had his young protégé leave. "Letty, take these travel documents to Mr. Edelman on Vestingstraat. He needs them right now."

Letty ran out the front door. Workers sang songs as they bent over their cutting and polishing benches. They belted songs out in unison while the traders, with a delicate touch, balanced their elaborate scales with boxes of tiny weights, each ensconced in its proper compartment. Letty weaved through the alleys lost in her daydreams. Mother took all of her earnings, counting it out on the kitchen table every payday, but Letty hid a small amount, enough to go to the movies every couple of weeks. Without telling her, Letty watched Alfred Hitchcock films and imagined herself breaking away from her family and dashing off to Hollywood and returning a huge success. Sometimes riding a white horse, other times a hot air balloon, and always her hair blowing in the wind.

In the hot and humid streets she pushed through lunch crowds. She turned down a backstreet to get off the main road deciding to twist her way towards the Central Train station away from the hoards of people and out of the sun. Letty thought she knew the way, but before she realized it she was lost in a maze of back alleys she'd never seen. She walked by fire escapes and laundry lines looking for a way back to the main street. Over her shoulder there was a group of boys pacing her. The hair on her neck stood up.

Letty saw the end of the alley. The group was gaining on her now only fifty feet behind. The bright light of the street ahead was at least 40 yards away. She didn't dare run, but quickened her pace.

One of the boys called out, "Hey, girl!"

"I'm late for Hebrew school," she said not wanting to show fear. It was the first thing she thought to say.

"Stop for second!" the boy called again.

Three of the boys split off and went down a narrow path and the boy who called to her continued to follow closing the distance between them.

Soon the boy moved next to her, shoulder to shoulder. He was taller and older and wore a white collared shirt. He wasn't a poor boy. She kept her eyes focused on the bright street ahead and shifted the leather satchel of documents and tightened her grip.

"You have 50 centimes?" the boy asked. "I'm thirsty."

Letty didn't respond. She had no money, but she also didn't want to provoke him. Letty stared ahead and was getting closer to the bright light. He locked stride with her.

"You have 50 centimes you Jew?" he said. "You freeloading Jew!

Coming here and taking it all for yourself! I've got a knife I'm going to stick you! I'm going to stick you! You Jew!"

She said nothing. The Flemish National League in Antwerp had grown anti-Semitic with the rise of Hitler to the East and there were stories about Jews stealing jobs. She knew the boy was working himself up to do something.

Letty's mind zipped through the options: Run now and he grabs her; keep a fast walk and stall his attack; hit him with the satchel and run; or she could start yelling. She was almost at the street and her eyes adjusted to the bright light. She saw people walking, but needed to time it right.

Her knuckles flexed around the satchel. In a split second she swung the ledger up as hard as her arms allowed smashing them into the boy's face. She sprinted begging her legs to run faster and faster. She heard foot falls behind her gaining, and terror pooled in her stomach. In that small eternity she was running in place. She opened her mouth and nothing came out. She tried again and nothing.

Then finally she heard her voice. She screamed and screamed.

People on the street stopped and looked down the alley and saw her break into the light. Gasping she ran up to a man and looked back, but didn't see the boy.

Coming around the corner was the group of boys up the street that had split off in the alley. They turned around seeing the crowd and ducked into another alleyway. "What is it girl? Are you okay?"

"Someone was chasing me," she said. "I'm okay. I'm okay. I need to get to my job." She slipped through the crowd with her heart thundering in her ears and adrenaline rushing from the tussle with the boy, and now also worried she wouldn't complete Mr. Behr's task. She looked over her shoulder, but they were gone.

5

Double back.

It wasn't the boys in the alley that jeopardized Letty's job; it turned out it was Annie's best friend. Toby Lerner forgot to button the top of her blouse, her skirt was tight and she wore black stockings and bright red lipstick. She squeezed Letty's arm like a doll when she came into the office. "Annie mentioned you worked here."

"I'll show you around," Letty said.

"Oh, no need," Toby said. "Mr. Behr said he would do that."

She turned her back on Letty and struck up a conversation with the accountant, a young man happy to oblige. Toby's laugh was loud and her voice carried through the small office. Letty loved her job, and that changed the day Toby started working at the travel agency.

Mr. Behr gave Toby the departure and arrival times to post, which was about the only thing she did. But Toby also took control of the delivery and pick-up logs ordering Letty to do the routes she didn't want. Usually the ones that were far and out of the way. "Letty, go down to Londenstraat to pick up the shipping times," Toby said. "Did you hear me? I need you to do it now. And deliver these tickets too."

The harbor was a good distance away and Letty had a stack of work Mr. Behr put on her desk. Yet since Toby was new Letty picked up the shipping times from the cruise line companies for her, made the deliveries, and stayed late to finish diamond appraisal paperwork. Then the next day she ordered Letty to do it again. When it happened the day after that it was apparent she thought her job was to order Letty to do the work she didn't want.

"What's the matter Letty?" Toby said as Letty stepped into the office from her deliveries, out of breath.

Letty showed her the misprinted names she caught on a ship voyage ticket to New York and had rushed back. Toby plucked the documents from her and walked them to Leon Stolar, the second in charge at the agency.

"There's a problem with these tickets," she said. "The names are misspelled." But forgot to mention Letty found the error.

"Good catch," he said.

"Looks like Toby is fitting in nicely," Mr. Behr said, poking his head out of his office. His words were like screeching metal on Letty's ears.

It was only a matter of time before the luster of Toby's veneer rubbed off. Letty first noticed an inaccuracy on the departure board. Then she looked closer and they were all off by an hour. Every one. Trips that said noon departures to New York should have been eleven. If the times on the board weren't correct, the tickets that were booked weren't correct. It was a huge mistake. But instead of fixing them Letty waited for Mr. Behr to notice, and it didn't take long.

"These departure times are all wrong!" Mr. Behr said. His voice boomed through the office. "Who did these? They need to be fixed right now! What are we waiting for?"

No one said anything, or moved. He asked again, his voice louder than Letty ever heard. Toby kept her head down.

"It's crucial that you post accurate information!" he said walking toward Toby. There was sweat on his forehead and he wiped his nose. "Our business depends on it!"

"Yes, sorry, sir," Toby said and nodded toward Letty. "But I only posted the information that Letty gave me."

Mr. Behr turned his attention in Letty's direction. She swallowed, but it didn't help the tickle that itched her dry throat. She waited for him with her sweaty palms flat on the table. As soon as he started for

16

Letty she saw Toby combing her desk for the paperwork, the evidence, which needed to be discarded. The office was silent watching the whole scene unfold. Usually Letty left the shipping schedules with Toby. But seeing they were wrong on the public boards she doubled back that morning and grabbed the original paperwork off Toby's desk while she was flirting with the accountant. She knew how Toby operated and it was Letty's job to copy the times from the dockyard's schedule. She was on the hook if they were written wrong, especially if Toby discarded the proof.

"Letty, what do you say for yourself?" Mr. Behr said. His hands were in his pockets as he rocked on the heels of his loafers.

"I have the times right here," Letty said and handed them to him. Toby stopped searching and her head snapped up. He looked them over and nodded dropping the paper back on her desk.

"From now on you will post the departure and arrival times," he said. "You will also double check the delivery logs." He returned to his dimly lit office.

"It was Letty's fault," Toby said to the accountant, and then the receptionist, trying to plead her case. "She's the one with the wrong information."

"Sorry, honey," the receptionist said in her falsetto voice. "I don't make the rules here." Toby was gone within the week.

6

Find the edge pieces.

California

Grandma needed to use the bathroom so I stopped recording. "It's terrible getting old," she said. "I have all these problems the doctors can't figure out. I'll be back, my dear boy." Her feet tested the floor the same as a baby learning to walk, but she found her footing and moved over the carpet at a slow and concentrated pace. In that brief moment I thought back to the linoleum floor deep in my memory.

I stepped and jumped from square to square down a long, sterile corridor, my focus intense not to touch the lines in between the white linoleum tiles. People dressed in blue brushed by. Someone nudged my shoulders forward, and out of the way. At the end of the hallway a large window filled the hall with bright summer sun. I saw a figure by the window dressed in a jungle-patterned frock. It was grandma. That was my first memory of her and it was from a day I wish I could erase.

Grandma stared out at the palm trees swaying in the California breeze and a seagull bouncing up and down in the air currents. Her eyes turned up to the clock and its hands stuttering on the hospital wall.

I ran past her not saying a word and through a door to my mother's open arms. Tubes taped into place channeled liquid to pouches and monitors. "My little *bubala*," mom said, kissing me on the forehead and squeezing me with a weak hug careful not to tangle me in the cords and the tape that connected them to her.

I handed her felt pens and a piece of paper and watched her draw the outline of a perfect galloping horse. I took it and began to color it in.

I didn't notice the bandana covering mom's head. She always wore one. That or a brown wig. I felt her eyes watching me and I looked at her smile, but I thought nothing of it and returned my attention to my picture.

Before I finished putting the streaks on the horse's mane a screen started beeping. From the corner of my eye I saw grandma point to me. Her fingers waved toward the door and someone's hands grabbed my arms. I threw them off, but they kept tugging. I swung and kicked. Tears filled up my eyes as large hands gripped my arms like a straitjacket.

"I don't want to go, not yet! Mom!" She sat there smiling at me. I twisted breaking out of the tight grasp and I lunged close to her. It was like someone else spitting on her. Beads of my saliva sprayed her face. She blinked, but didn't try to get out of the way, only smiled at me, who had just spit in her face.

"I love you my little *bubala*," she said as I was hoisted onto a shoulder and the white linoleum squares raced past below me. My cries echoed down the hospital walls as if they were someone else's wails. It was the last time I ever saw my mom and life became very blurred.

"I can't believe you!" my dad said in a quiet and snarling voice into the phone. "I received the notice from your lawyer. How can you take away Aaron's home? Our home. We are living in a one bedroom apartment for Christ sake!" His eyes bulged, veins swelled around his neck, and his face grew scarlet red. "What about Aaron? Is this what you want for him?"

I heard grandma's voice come through the phone, but I couldn't hear what she was saying.

"You did this, Letty —" dad said.

He abruptly stopped trying to get his words in—was resigned to listen.

"So Karin wants her son's house *to be sold?*" dad said. "Her wishes... You want to honor your daughter's wishes by taking her son's home?...a trust for when he is 18, what good is that now?"

Grandma's voice was piercing through the phone. The effect on my dad was like a stab to the gut.

"We were divorced!" he said. "But—"

There was a loud click and then the buzzing of a dial tone.

Months later I was sent to visit Grandma in Palo Alto. The child psychologist suggested it would help "process" the loss, but I didn't know the exact reason. Perhaps lawyers arranged it. All I knew was that grandma was trying to take my house, the house that I once lived in with my mom.

A black and white TV played a Spanish telanovela in the kitchen. Grandma was practicing Spanish. It was the first time I had seen her since my mom died. "Awww, my boy, *mi nieto*, you have grown! Come in and let's put your things down."

I scanned the wall hangings, black and white photos, foreign rugs, shelves of books, exotic statues and old charms. Though the smells of spices and foods were different from anything I'd ever known, somehow they reminded me of my mom.

"These are my favorite," Grandma said handing me a caramel. "You have a birthday coming? How old will you be?"

"Eight."

"Do you miss your mom, Sweets? How are you doing?" I nodded, yes. "Is there anything I can do?"

"I wish she had a place where I could visit her," I said. "In the cemetery."

"We planted a tree in her honor in that nice park. She wanted to be cremated."

I looked at my grandma confused as to why anyone would want to be cremated. I wanted to scream at her about why she left me no place to visit my mom and why I never got to say goodbye.

"Cremation is when your body is turned to ashes and returned to the earth," grandma said. I knew what it was and I hated the idea of it. All I could think of was my mom's body being shoved into a flaming oven.

"What did they do with her ashes?"

"Her friends took them out on a boat and scattered them in the ocean."

"But now she's completely gone."

"You have the tree, Aaron," Grandma said. "These were your mom's wishes." Grandma paused and dabbed the creases at the corners of her lips with a tissue.

We sat at the kitchen table in silence staring at puzzle pieces she scattered on the table. Some of the edge pieces were connected.

"Look for the edges," Grandma said pushing her small hands through the pieces. "It makes for an easier time." I stared at the bits on the table but sat still.

"Are you American?" I finally asked. I was nervous grandma wasn't American. She was so different from my other grandparents. The way she talked and the different languages she spoke when she answered the phone. The foreign things that hung on the walls in her house. The strange smells.

"I am. But I was born in Berlin, Germany, and grew up in Antwerp. Do you know where those places are?"

I didn't. "Is that why you have an accent?"

"No, that's the cigarettes. Don't you ever start smoking or you'll speak like this." Grandma chuckled and stared at her wall of pictures. She smiled and got up, pulling over a large world globe. "You know, *boychick*, you and I are very similar. Have you heard much about World War II?"

I nodded.

"You have? What a smart kid. How do you know about it?"

"I've seen *The Longest Day* and I know they defeat the Nazis," I said.

"I watch it every time it's on TV. John Wayne movies are my favorite."

"Ha! John Wayne! Of course. I like Hitchcock, personally. Do you know him?" I didn't.

"My mom drew me horses. Can you draw horses like her?"

"No, I'm sorry, my dear. Your mom was a wonderful artist. I don't have that talent."

"Do you like baseball?" I asked. "It's my favorite sport."

"I've never seen it," she said. "I'm afraid I don't know much about sports." Grandma shook her head and wiped the corners of her tight lips and waited for the kettle to boil.

"I'm sure John Wayne showed what an evil man Hitler was," she said as she poured hot water into two mugs for tea. "Here's some sugar cubes. I like to dip them." She let one soak up the tea and then sucked on it. "World War II was a terrible time. It was bad, like what you are going through now."

"Were you in World War II?" I asked. She nodded, yes. That surprised me. My grandma didn't seem like a person that fought in the war. Only men were soldiers, like John Wayne.

"Yes, it was awful," grandma said as she ran her fingers over the mass of colorful puzzle pieces. "When your world is falling apart, all you can do is look for the edge pieces to make sense of the chaos. Did you also know your family was Jewish?"

I shook my head. I didn't know what a Jew was, but I didn't think I was one.

"Are you Jewish?" I asked.

"Short answer is, yes, my *boychick*," she said. "The Jewish religion is passed down through the mother. So your mother was Jewish too."

"Am I Jewish?"

"You are."

"But I'm Catholic and Irish."

"So you're an Irish, Catholic, Jew," she said setting tea down and poking me in the arm. "Well, I don't believe in religion anyway. What has it done for us? So let me tell you the story about why I have this

22

accent."

She rotated the globe and pointed to Palo Alto, where we sat, and then to Europe and began her story.

7

No good thing lasts forever.

Antwerp, Belgium

Police patrolled out front of Letty's apartment building. She ran up the stairs and into the flat sidestepping Mrs. Rheinholt, a tenant with a nose that hung to her chin, to whom their mother rented a room for extra money. "I ought to bop you girl for startling me," she said as she steadied herself on the wall creating a trail of grease smudges.

Aromas wafted from the kitchen and Letty heard the pans clinking. Mother was cooking the feast for Seder. In the living room sitting on a small wooden chair was a man. Letty had to look away and then back again to make sure her eyes weren't playing tricks. It was father!

"My little *bubala*," Aron said. "It's me!" She became conscious of her appearance and rubbed the wrinkles out of her dress and flicked her hair from her eyes. Father held his arms out and she ran over to hug him. It was over four years since she had seen him. He looked thinner and his long beard was greying. There were more wrinkles around his eyes.

Annie peered out the window holding the drapes back a smidge. Father smuggled himself into the country from the Netherlands under the blanket of a horse cart for Passover, bringing with him chocolates and candies from Amsterdam, which Suzy took from him, offering the sweets to her sisters with a magnanimous smile.

There was a constant flow of police on the street. Father had a warrant for his arrest and if the police caught him he would go to jail. So each daughter took turns keeping lookout.

Mother's lips were firm as she looked over the table. She made sure all the proper dishes were prepared: matzo, a bone of lamb, an egg, lettuce, salt water, charoset (a mixture of apples, nuts, cinnamon and wine) sat on a kosher plate, and four cups of wine plus an extra for prophet Elijah. The girls drank a special raisin wine mother made, but tonight they had a glass of the real stuff too.

Father was at the head of the table in a large chair conducting the Seder as he had always done, wearing his furry *shtreimel* hat and dark suit. Mother and Annie brought the steaming food to the table and Letty ran back and forth to the window watching for police.

"Take them out of the land of Egypt; this night is the Lord's, guarding all the children of Israel throughout their generations," father's voice shook as he read the passage from *Exodus*. Letty saw mother look over her family and show the faintest of smiles. Her wig's curls drooped over her shoulders.

Letty gasped. There were two policemen walking up the front stairs of their apartment building and they entered the lobby door.

"Police came into the building," she said from the window. Everyone turned toward the door and father looked at Letty with his soft eyes. Both Suzy and Annie joined her at the window and mother walked to the front door. Voices drifted up from the ground floor and creaking floors resonated in the silence of the apartment.

The police stepped back down the stairs closing the lobby door behind them with cigarettes lit and strolled off into the night inhaling the smoke of their rollups. Before the family returned to their seats father continued reciting from *Exodus*.

"An avenging angel went from house to house killing every first-born son," he said. "But sparing the Israelites." Father grinned at his family finding humor in the irony of the moment. He was a pious man.

Normally Letty wanted Passover to be over as soon as it started. She preferred the Harvest Festival to all the killing and massacres, but this night—this Passover—was different. As the minutes ticked away, she became greedy for every second wishing for a divine intervention to allow him to stay, to let the Seder continue on.

"God, freeze this moment and let us bask in it a little longer," she said a prayer to herself. Father performed the Seder well past 1:00 in the morning. Then he got up from his chair and she knew he was going to leave.

"I love you my *bubala*," he said squeezing Annie against his chest. She held onto him not letting go and tears flowed down her cheeks. She buried her face into his shoulder breathing in the musty smell of his coat. He rubbed her back humming a prayer. Letty's eyes also filled with tears and she hugged him.

Father set his mink *shtreimel* in its box and handed it to mother replacing it with his wide-brimmed hat. Mother handed him a small bag of food. Her face was resigned allowing little emotion, but Letty thought she saw her eyes mist over. Father was leaving for Poland to see his ailing mother.

They watched him make his way down the stairs one step at a time. He looked up and waved as he walked out the lobby door. He vanished into the night as if he were never there.

After father disappeared into the blackness of the street Letty went into the bathroom. She sat on the toilet. It was quiet throughout the house, except she heard mother cleaning in the kitchen.

Mother was adamant that her daughters never utter "God" in the bathroom. "He will strike you down right there," she told Letty when she was five. For years Letty feared her words. Now she didn't see why God's ears were open in the bathroom, but not anywhere else? God didn't seem to listen, not even to the small, yet reasonable request to let father stay with them.

She sat there trying to face what she already knew to be true in her heart. So she said it. "God." She said it so quietly that she almost didn't hear herself say it. Her eyes shut bracing for something, a fate she didn't know. She knew a lightning strike was a childish exaggeration, yet maybe a piece of the wall or a pipe might fall on her?

There was nothing and she sat on the toilet staring into the abyss of the bathroom's cracked wall. "God," she said louder goading Him to do His worst. But again, nothing. "God, did you hear me? I piss on you! I piss on you!" she said just loud enough so mother didn't hear. Only the clanking of pots in the kitchen disturbed the peace of the apartment. Father left her that night for the last time, but like a ringmaster packing up the circus and moving to the next city, so did God.

8

Some know better than others. Listen to them.

Aron's letters sat on the kitchen table, and they were all that remained of him in the apartment. Only Annie continued her Torah study with Sulamith Ostersetzer, a refugee from Germany. She was one of a 100,000 Jews to flee the German Reich a few years earlier.

It seemed Mrs. Ostersetzer understood Nazi aggression better than others. When news headlines told of the non-aggression pact Germany signed with Russia, she knew Poland (where Aron stayed with his parents, stuck ever since his passport expired) was now in the crosshairs of Hitler. She watched closely because she knew that once Poland fell, Belgium and the Netherlands would be next.

"If that happens, I don't know where to go. France, England?" she said. Yet, that all seemed so implausible to the Schmidt family, who didn't pay as close attention and also didn't understand the warning signals as she did. Annie just heard her commentary in passing.

Mrs. Ostersetzer had streaks of grey hair. Her house was lined with religious texts and scrolls, though most of her possessions remained in Germany, either destroyed or sold in the name of the Fuhrer. She saw the writing on the wall as the Nazi party took rights away from Jews. She fled Germany to Belgium in one of the first waves. The Reich encouraged Jews to emigrate at first, but as the years wore on they made Jews leave most of their money and valuables behind. Mrs. Ostersetzer crossed the border with as many books as she could stuff in her suitcases. Her family and friends clung to their homes in Germany saying they would ride this turbulent wave until it "eventually" passed.

In Antwerp Mrs. Ostersetzer continued her study of the Torah. Rabbis debated the merits of translating the Torah into other languages like German saying in all their high-mindedness, "The truth of the Torah will be translated incorrectly." But Mrs. Ostersetzer believed her young students gained a wider understanding from the labor.

"Annie, the meaning of this verse in Hebrew is different in your translation. Do you know why the German means something else?" Annie bit on her pencil and pushed her bangs behind her ears checking over the passage and erasing the mistake. Quiet and astute, Annie was one of her star pupils.

One day Mrs. Ostersetzer put a hand on Annie's shoulder as she thumbed through a German dictionary. She never touched her students, and now this unexpected contact alarmed Annie.

"The radio reported that Germany invaded Poland," Mrs. Ostersetzer said. Annie's eyes snapped up to her teacher.

"My father is in Poland," Annie said. "Will he be okay?"

"I don't know." Mrs. Ostersetzer had seen the Nazis through her apartment window years earlier harassing Jews on the street, and had little faith in the benevolent treatment of people in Poland, let alone Jews.

Russia also invaded Poland. The Germans and Russia split the country in two. There was a chance Aron was on the side controlled by Russia, which meant he had a better chance.

"What do we do?" Annie said. She stuffed her books and belongings into a bag and walked toward the door looking at Mrs. Ostersetzer for direction.

"If they invade Belgium, leave. Leave fast. Don't wait."

Annie rushed home with the news. Her eyes were red and puffy but she didn't cry in front of the family. "Poland is now occupied by

Germany." Mother had little reaction, though Suzy looked upset.

The radio said cities were bombed and shipping harbors were blockaded by the Nazis. Annie and Letty looked over the maps but there was no clear evidence where German control ended and Russian control started. There just wasn't enough information in newspapers. It looked as if Ranizow where father lived with his parents sat right on the dividing line between the Russians and Germans. Which country had control was hard to tell. They hoped he was on the Russian side.

A letter came from father a few days later. Mother tore at its seam and pulled out and unfolded the creased letter. She read it and handed it to Annie. "He's okay," mother said. "Your *babushka* is getting better."

"He didn't mention the German invasion—" Annie said.

"It was written before," Suzy said.

Tears streamed down Annie's face as the realization that they probably wouldn't see him again resonated. Mother pulled out cabbage and beef for stew and stared at Annie, who hid her eyes.

"Why the tears?" mother asked. "He wrecked the family. Be thankful you have a roof and food to eat. I don't want to see you crying about this anymore. Enough." Annie wiped her eyes and set the table with mother's kosher plates.

It was the last letter they received from father.

9

Nothing is what it seems.

Havana, Cuba

She was getting old and it was the urge to impress grandma that I said, "yes," to the trip. A group of Mormon missionaries I met a week earlier after I arrived in Mexico to learn Spanish during college proposed the idea of going to Cuba. At the time Americans were banned from travelling to the communist, island country.

So when I found myself walking in a complete daze through the crumbling streets of Havana, Cuba, a city whose grandeur hid behind years of neglect and sanctions, the line between reality and the surreal was thin. A week earlier I hadn't even thought of such a journey. Now I was greedily soaking up every bit of scenery, smell, and sound. I just couldn't get enough of the thick Caribbean air, the pastel colors that adorned the chipped stucco on the old Cubana buildings, and the old Chevy and Pontiac cars that made you feel as if you were in a 50's time warp.

In the streets of Havana, we stirred curious interest from everyone we passed: men working on *carcachas* (junker cars) with hopes of resurrection, old women clad in purple and pink spandex sweeping their porches clean of debris, and of course the children who were consumed with their passion, *béisbol*.

Cubans and Americans have a common love, and that is baseball.

On almost every Havana street, walled in by buildings that once were beautiful but now stand battered and weathered by the salty air, you can hear the howls of kids playing stickball and dodging cars. Here, *béisbol* is king of the street.

As we passed through the *calles* commandeered for the ball games, the bright smiles on the children's faces and the screams of enjoyment were just too hard to resist. All it took that day were a few enthusiastic words in my broken Spanish, "*podemos jugar con ustedes?*" and before we knew it, the famous baseball rivalry, America versus Cuba was taking center stage on a street in Havana.

The excitement was visible on every person's face. Our Cuban counterparts, 12 to 17 year old boys dressed in tank tops and shorts, tried but could not restrain their immense pride in representing their country, in what I guess can be compared to as the World Series of stickball. All the men working on their *carcachas* left them for another day, the old women put down their brooms, little giggling girls began to congregate, and the laundry lines that hung from the windows were now replaced with upperdeck seating as the balconies came alive with people. A small crowd had begun to surround this urban field.

The ballpark boundaries were laid out: any ball hit before the tan apartment and through windows was out of play, three pitches and you're out, and if you hit it over the fence or past the street lamp, home run. And with those directions, the game was on.

I was nervous. I hadn't swung a bat, or in this case a stick, since I was cut from the college baseball team two years earlier. And the Cubans, who have produced some of baseball's most talented athletes, were the opposition. So I gingerly stepped up to the rusty tin pan that served as home plate, took a few practice swings, and assumed my batting stance. The pitcher, a large, muscular sixteen-year-old stared in at me, and I can only imagine what he thought of the sunburned *gringo* that he was now facing.

With a smile he wound up and fired in the baseball, a tightly rolled ball of tape that danced in the air. Thinking I was He-Man, or more likely showing off for the crowd, I took an enormous rip with my weapon, and hit nothing but air. The spectators howled and shouted out words of encouragement—for me, I think. Determined not to look like a fool I took my batting stance once again. I focused in on that big kid, and he just smiled with a twinkle in his eye like he knew something I didn't.

Excited yells began coming from the balconies, "*cuidado! cuidado!*" and at that moment the pitcher and everyone else scattered to the door stoops, where I joined them just as a rusty blue 56 Chevy came barreling around the corner. With a honk, a wave, and a cloud of smoke it was gone, and the game was back.

As I waited again, poised with my stick, the pitcher sent the ball of tape speeding my way and I took another huge swing, this time whacking the ball with authority —it sliced into the street like a laser for a base hit. The crowd erupted with cheers, sending little shivers down my spine, and I stood on first base with a grin that stayed with me for the rest of the day. People were patting me on the back like I just did something great. And the pitcher smiled at me with that same twinkle in his eye.

It wasn't a competition; it was a treat for him and everyone else, including me. How often do we get to play stickball in the streets of Havana with the kids of Cuba, and how often do they get to play with the kids of America?

Months later I wrote my Cuba experience down, and "*Béisbol, Havana Style*" became my first published article in a newspaper. I was anxious to show grandma the clipping. I knew she related everything to the books she read. She once told me how she danced around one of her favorite authors, Thomas Friedman, when she bumped into him in an elevator. "Can you imagine this old woman acting like a teenager?" she said. I was eager to get her reaction to my story. Maybe even impress her. I studied her face as she read and she even chuckled as her eyes moved over the words.

"Sounds like a fun trip, my boy," was all she said and she set the clipping down next to her Barcalounger shuffling to the kitchen to put the kettle on. I picked it up folding the article and put it in my pocket, disappointed by her reaction. I don't know what I was looking for, what I wanted, yet I yearned for something.

The phone rang in her apartment and she started speaking French to the person on the other end. I didn't understand their conversation, but wondered about the world she came from.

10

Understand peoples' motives.

Antwerp, Belgium

Warplanes flew overhead on May 10, 1940 as Nazis invaded Belgium. Letty first heard their rumble and then their outlines chopping through the air above. It was Friday and Shabbat. The sky was dotted with them for as far as her eyes saw. They flew low and they flew high. People stopped in the streets and they all stood with their heads cocked to the sky. In the distance the explosions thundered as bombers let their payloads flutter to earth.

"Now I won't have to go to work!" was Letty's first thought. Her offices were closed and the owner, Mr. Behr, left for England. She ran through the streets all the way to the apartment weaving around people standing like statues and their tilted heads gazing at the clouds. She was out of breath, but her adrenaline was running on the excitement in the air. "War, I hope it's true."

Thousands of German planes bombed buildings and airfields around Antwerp and then German troops parachuted and glided down seizing bridges across the Albert Canal, which wound its way to Antwerp.[1] They were coming for them.

Letty was the last to make it home where Suzy and Annie sat by the kitchen table as mother paced. Their building manager confirmed to mother German ground forces entered Belgium at about six o'clock in

35

the morning, but were meeting Belgian resistance.

"Letty, what took you so long?" mother said. Her face was worried and she didn't know what to do. Letty walked into the middle of a debate; whether to stay or to flee Antwerp.

"I talked with a Belgian soldier," Suzy said. "Antwerp will be the safest place for us. He said the Germans wouldn't bomb it. Even if they take control of the city we can wait the war out in Antwerp. He thought we're better off staying. The Belgians will push them back. If we leave, who knows what there will be, or where to go."

"The Germans will put us in prisoner camps if they take over," Annie said. "We have to leave as soon as possible. The longer we wait the more chance we'll be trapped—"

"How do you know we won't be caught in the fighting if we leave?" Suzy said. "There are bombs being dropped everywhere! Most of them outside the city!" Mother stood watching them argue. She was paralyzed with indecision. Letty was quiet too. She was more interested in the spectacle transforming their dull lives into epic ones. "My sisters have more sense than me; they are frightened," she thought.

"Mrs. Ostersetzer left Germany because of how they treated Jews," Annie said. "Do you think they're going to be nice once they're in Antwerp? She's leaving tomorrow." Suzy's face turned beet red. She wanted to wallop Annie, but mother stepped in.

"It's Shabbat, we're not going anywhere, Annie," mother said, taking Suzy's side. Mother always sided with Suzy. As children, if Suzy ever wanted anything her sisters had, like a toy or clothes or candy, she only had to tell mother the item was "impure" for it to be confiscated and locked in her oak chest. Suzy wore the key for the lock around her neck.

"We can ask our neighbors what they're going to do," Letty said from the corner of the kitchen.

Mother glared at Letty as if she was stupid, but Suzy thought it was a chance to prove Annie wrong.

"Yes, let's ask our neighbors," Suzy said. Mother agreed.

"Hurry then," she said. They all left the apartment in a rush because it was the Sabbath and they needed to be home by sundown. Not because there was a marching army heading their direction.

Letty ran down the stairs and burst out onto the street. It was as if the ground was on fire as men and women picked their feet up helter-skelter not stopping for anything.

"Excuse me sir," she said to a Jewish man with long *peyos* twirling down his cheeks. He didn't stop and stepped around her. Everyone wanted to get home.

She saw a man that lived in their building. He didn't want to stop either, but did. His family was leaving in the morning. According to him trains were waiting at the main station to take refugees south into France. They were worried about German prisoner camps and didn't want to stick around to find out about the Nazis' plans.

Many of their neighbors feared German camps. Reports about how the Nazis treated Jews in Germany and Austria had filtered out. Most people were heading to the train station as soon as possible.

"It's irresponsible to leave our home so quick," Suzy said, pressing mother's buttons despite the consensus on the street. Mother was quick to agree. She loved her things and her life here was safe compared to the unknown. Only Annie was pushing to leave. Letty didn't have an opinion one-way or the other.

"We aren't going anywhere until after Shabbat," mother said. "Mrs. Weiner down the street said we can join them in their truck. They're going to the coast after the Sabbath." Until then the family was staying put, even as German Panzer and armored columns rolled toward Antwerp.

[1] Obermaier, Ernst (1989) *Die Ritterkreuztrager der Luftwaffe 1939-1945, Band I* (Verlag Dieter Hoffmann, Mainz).

11

Don't rush it.

Mother lit candles eighteen minutes before sunset marking the beginning of Shabbat. She recited the Kiddush over wine to sanctify Shabbat. In the middle of eating the stew she had prepared all day, air raid sirens went off.

"Let's go!" mother said. "Down to the cellar!" The white of her eyes showed the panic. None of them had ever been in such a situation. Mother, Suzy and Annie pushed their chairs back and ran down three flights of stairs letting their food sit. But Letty stayed and ate alone not wanting it to get cold. She was scraping her plate when the sirens ended and mother and her sisters climbed back up the stairs.

"You disrespectful snot!" she said. Blima's eyes were bulging and she smacked Letty hard on the back of the head. Her ears wrung from the thump. Blima straightened her *sheitel,* brushing the wig hair from her eyes. "How dare you disobey me! Have you any sense stupid girl. These bombs are real!"

The next morning the little temple was empty except for a handful of old women and the Schmidts, the rest making their escape. Letty looked at mother and wondered if she grasped what was coming their direction, because no one really knew. All Letty understood was that this dull life was about to be over. Forty minutes after sunset they performed the *Havdalah* ritual concluding Shabbat. Letty grabbed a suitcase and put a few changes of clothes and some books inside. She even applied some powder on her round cheeks and red lipstick.

Suzy laid her favorite clothes out and then unlocked her chest with the key around her neck. Inside were all sorts of treasures the years had accumulated including books, dolls and treats father once gave Annie and Letty. They lay squashed under the weight of Suzy's other possessions. It was the first time Letty was able to gaze into the forbidden region and most of it was untouched and in pristine condition. Suzy sifted through it but took only one thing, the padlock that secured the chest, leaving the rest for the Nazis.

Mother sat at the kitchen table sewing. When she was done she handed each girl a little bag with a strap.

"Put this around your neck," she said. "It's for your identity cards." Like little kids they put them on and slipped their passports in.

They stood in their apartment before the sun rose in the morning each holding a single suitcase. Mother's pictures hung on the walls; her vases, kosher plates, and embroidered furniture sat still in their places. Cranky Mrs. Rheinholt was long gone and the apartment was silent.

"Grab the alarm clock, Annie!" mother said, remembering one more thing she wanted to bring and stalling the inevitable.

Mother turned the lights out and the four of them walked down the dark street with their luggage. Despite the early hour the street was busy. Babies screamed on their mothers' backs and others pushed by in a hurry. When they arrived at Mrs. Weiner's building to catch a ride to the coast, it was still dark and there was no sign of a truck anywhere.

12

The best option isn't always best.

The apartment was a mess with open cupboards, drawers and papers littering the floor—its inhabitants had left in a rush. Mrs. Weiner was nowhere to be found.

"She left us," mother said in shock. "Did I get the time right?" On the verge of tears, she muttered to herself. A man peered through curtains at them on the front steps of the building.

"We need to catch a train south," Annie said. "We shouldn't wait much longer." Annie was anxious to leave Antwerp after Mrs. Ostersetzer's stark warning. A door opened on the ground floor.

"Can I help you?" a man said. He spoke Flemish and mother didn't understand. She looked at him with a blank gaze.

"We're looking for Mrs. Weiner," Annie said. "We were supposed to meet her. Do you know where she is?"

"Ask him where they are!" mother said, becoming more frantic.

"She just did," Letty said.

He looked down and started shaking his head. The street lamp cast shadows deep in the crevices of his parched mouth. The morning birds began to sing around them.

The man's eyes filled with tears as he told the story that he had just learned hours earlier. The old man had known Mrs. Weiner and her family for decades. They left yesterday to catch the refugee boats to England. One of which was a boat Letty's family were supposed to catch with them.

Mrs. Weiner's family took the truck late in the evening to Knokke-Heist, 60 miles north of Dunkirk, on the coast. The drive was a little over an hour and the family waited on the beach throughout the night until early morning. The refugee boats didn't come as scheduled and they stood in the sand straining their eyes over the vast ocean in hopes that something would appear in the western horizon. The sun rose to the east and they became uneasy. They heard the buzz of warplanes above and daylight was exposing them on the shore.

"There's a boat!" one of the refugees yelled and pointed north. Instead of an evacuation boat coming over the horizon, it was a German *Schnellboot* cruising along the coast about 100 feet off the beach. Their sailors stared at them. The boat slowed and then stopped. They saw they were refugees with suitcases, but the sailors pulled the bolts on their large mounted machine guns. In an instant the sand kicked up around them and bullets whizzed past as fire spewed from the tips of the guns. The rapid cracks and booms of gunfire resounded in their ears as they realized they were being fired on. They scattered to the dunes and by the time the refugees took cover, two of Mrs. Weiner's children were among the dozens sprawled out dead on the beach.

"I loved those kids," the old man said. He shook his head and wiped his tears. Mrs. Weiner was still on the coast burying her children, but the driver of the truck had returned with the news, and to pick up more people. The old man, overtaken by his emotions, shut the door without any further words.

"We must go to the train station," Annie said to mother.

"It's too dangerous to travel right now!" Suzy said. "Did you not hear what this man just said?" Mother nodded her head. With whom she agreed, Annie or Suzy, Letty didn't know (or, couldn't guess).

"What about Bernard?" Letty said. Their cousin Bernard lived nearby. He had helped them move their furniture when father fled Belgium years earlier. "He might have a plan or information."

41

It was somewhere to go, away from the old man's story. They didn't say a word to each other as the crisp morning air cut into thoughts. Mother was crying, Letty suspected for all that she was leaving behind, or, for Mrs. Weiner. Letty didn't feel anything but the coldness of the morning breeze.

She knocked on Bernard's door. There was no answer. They heard a radio playing inside, but there was no other noise. Letty knocked again. Nothing. As they turned to walk down the stairs a young man wearing a stocking cap bounded up the steps with a bag on his shoulder. It was Bernard.

"Auntie, I thought you were leaving for the coast?" Bernard said. "You're lucky to catch me. I'm leaving for the train station with my friend, Leo. I forgot some photos."

In his apartment the radio reported that Belgian forces fell at Fort Eben-Emael and it was a matter of time before the German's 18th Army broke through into Antwerp. Refugees were flooding to the train station. "Antwerp is under full evacuation before the Germans seal off exit routes and enter the city."

Letty felt a sense of urgency as inertia was peeled away and replaced with panic. They dashed down the stairs with Bernard and towards the central train station through side streets of the diamond-district. The shops where Letty had once made deliveries for Behr were closed and empty, and the streets were packed with people lugging their possessions. As they got closer to the station the street turned into a great flowing river of humans. Letty grabbed onto hands and arms of her sisters and Bernard. They held each other tight so they wouldn't be pulled off into another direction and lost forever.

People were screaming, some frantically looking for lost children, yet the flow wouldn't and couldn't stop for them. They tried to move back against the exodus, but they were swept back up into the torrent of people, the terror in their screams impossible to alleviate. There was no reasoning with the pandemonium. Holding hands soon wasn't enough and Letty locked arms with Annie and Bernard. Luggage and body parts got caught on mailboxes, light poles, parked cars and Letty kept breaking it free. They moved towards the station as the ocean of refugees crushed against each other and pushed through the doors of the opulent station. Letty shoved forward searching for the trains and the platforms. It was hard to see through the people. They were a few specs among thousands and thousands.

They pressed their way towards the stairs leading to the trains. Suzy led the way followed by mother, Annie, Letty and then Bernard and Leo. As they reached the bottom of the stairway congested with frantic refugees and their baggage, a large man blocked Bernard, holding him back so his own wife and children could move forward. Letty felt her arm pull and stretch, but she squeezed it tight, trying to pull Bernard past the man. She looked up and saw the man's jaw muscles flex in the thrashing sea of people. Nothing was going to get by him. She pulled again and then pleaded with him to let her cousin pass. "This is my cousin you are blocking," she said. "Let him by."

He shook his head without saying a word. They were deadlocked and the flow of people was pulling her. Her only choice was to let go of Annie, or Bernard. She let go of Bernard knowing it was probably the last time she'd see him. He smiled and put his hand up. The gush of people swept her up, and Bernard disappeared from sight.

Belgian police pushed them onto the platforms like cattle. Trains steamed into the station with railcars for as far as Letty's eyes saw. The noise was deafening and drowned out all thoughts. There was a puff of smoke and when it cleared a railcar with a few windows stood. A door at each end of the train car swung open and soldiers started pushing refugees in. The mass of people surged towards the closest car, pulling bags and children with them. She felt the policeman's hands on her back shoving her into the train, and before she knew it the light of the station was replaced by the dimness of the railcar.

Along the aisle were seats where grandmothers, grandfathers and small children sat. More and more refugees were pushed onto the trains and space became filled with nothing but bodies crammed together, with elbows, shoulders, knees, and faces all unceremoniously crushed together. The soldiers kept shoving people in until there was no more room to pack people standing up. Mother's eyes scanned for seats and found an old man that made room for her. Letty was unable to move, jammed between people and baggage. Their train car seemed to be filled with nothing but Jews. By the time the train started rolling there wasn't an inch to spare. They lurched forward to an unknown destination.

The train picked up speed and whistled. Letty looked through the twisting bodies to see out the window as heads, arms, torsos bobbed in the way. She glimpsed the outskirts of Antwerp, the villages and then grassy hills and trees. Letty closed her eyes and listened to a baby crying and then fell asleep standing up sandwiched between strangers.

13

Create space.

Loud explosions woke her. A German Stuka dive-bomber screamed overhead, unloading bombs. Their train rattled with the curvatures of the track and the reverberation of the shells. Letty looked around trying to orient herself.

"Get on the floor!" a man yelled. "Get away from the windows!"

Everyone piled into the aisle, knocking her down. She fell to the bottom crammed under a heap of men, women and children. They all scrambled and dug for the safety of the train's floor like a net of fish writhing for survival, but with nowhere to go. Letty tried to breathe but the wind was knocked from her under the crushing weight. She gasped for air and thought she was going to suffocate. Then the train stopped.

There was yelling in French. A man barked for them to take cover outside of the train. Refugees got off of her and she pulled herself up and climbed over suitcases. They poured out of the train cars. Mother didn't understand French.

"Run mother!" Letty said. "The man said run and take cover!"

They ran for a berm thirty yards from the train. Letty ran hard grabbing mother's arm and her dress and dove into the grass and dirt. Oxygen finally reached her lungs. The last car of the train caught fire and men were trying to put it out. They threw buckets of water from a cistern along the track. She looked down the rolling green fields at the hundreds of refugees hiding in the weeds and tall grass. The drone of warplanes above was a reminder that they made easy targets.

A minute later a man waved his arms begging them to hurry back to the train. Letty lifted mother up and they ran back with the hundreds of others somehow repacking themselves into the train.

"I told you we would be caught in the fighting if we left Antwerp!" Suzy said. "No one listened." She hit Annie on the back of her head. Annie was silent and held onto a strap that dangled from the train's wood paneled ceiling like a lifeless shank of meat.

Bombs fell nearer to the train with every pass of the planes. Mother moaned in terror, the lights flickered, and the train started moving again. Letty wasn't able to see the dive-bombers as hard as she strained her neck and eyes, but she heard their engines. It was difficult to tell if they were trying to hit them or just the tracks.

Another loud explosion and they piled onto the floor of the train. Letty was prepared this time and boxed out space in the pile with her elbows protecting her stomach and head. They stayed on the floor for hours feeling the bumps and vibrations of the train track, and explosions. Not one person knew where they were going. Only that they were heading south, into France.

14

Manage expectations.

There was one overflowing toilet of sewage spilling out onto the floor for the two hundred people in the train car. Each day it became worse. The Belgian army was forced to withdraw from Antwerp on May 16th and the Nazis entered the city days after the Schmidt family escaped on the train south. Still, Suzy was adamant they made a mistake fleeing, and the condition on the train reinforced her belief. It was a dirty mess of human sweat, saliva, tears, vomit, urine and feces that formed a stench that Letty's nose struggled to ignore.

"I'm going to be sick," mother said. "We should've never left. The filth is going to kill us. What were we thinking?" But neither she, nor Suzy thought about the Nazi army that had entered Antwerp. Then again, no one *really* knew about the Nazis.

The going was slow and the train stopped often encountering sections of track blown up by the Germans. The train reversed and traveled backwards towards Antwerp for what seemed like hours, searching for connecting track. When they found track the sentiment in the train car was of relief and excitement. They waited while the conductors manually changed the connectors to the new section of track, and then they slowly built up speed heading south again, thankful some breeze made it into the sweltering car. People cheered the train engineer for his improvisation.

Once again, they came up against bombed out track and the process started all over as the train backtracked. The sentiment in the car became depressed and fearful that maybe this would be the time that they wouldn't be able to find tracks south and the advancing German army moving swiftly would overtake them. It was like one of those bad dreams when you are being chased and running in thick mud. As hard as you move your legs and pump your arms the evil mass on your heels is about to swallow you up and there is nothing you can do. Mother's fear turned to tears when they came to a stop and started backwards. She looked around trying to see outside and then to each daughter.

"We've stopped," she said, her face hot and frantic. Then after a few minutes of waiting they felt the train under their feet rocking and the countryside outside moving in the opposite way and a barn they already passed going by. "It's the wrong direction," her eyes tearing up. Mother wanted to arrive somewhere, perhaps anywhere. The problem was they were stuck on the train with no end in sight and an advancing army dropping bombs all around.

"It's okay mother," Annie said. "We'll find a track."

"We'll get to France soon," Letty said.

"Will you two clean that toilet?" Suzy said. "Can you guarantee we won't be hit by a bomb? No! It's your fault we're in this mess! It's your fault mother is suffering like this!"

Mother sat stuffed in the middle of a man and woman with sagging faces and missing teeth. Mother's face was still fresh by comparison and she still wore her *scheitel*. She clung to it even though the wig trapped her body heat and soaked up perspiration in the baking temperature of the train car. She refused to take it off.

15

Set aside differences.

Palo Alto, CA

There was a picture frame of my mother when she was 12 wearing a cowboy hat sitting on a dresser, other than that the room was bare. My eyes shot around to the dark corners and edges of the room worried they might spy the ghost of my mom. It was my first visit since my mom died and grandma left the door ajar so some light trickled in.

Grandma's room was next to mine and reminded me of a jail cell. Her space was just big enough to fit a twin bed and a desk where she wrote letters. I listened to the clanks of her typewriter and Spanish dialogue filtered through the door into mine. On the other side of my room, was my grandfather's bedroom. He didn't' say much to me. "How are you, young chap?" he said in a posh English accent, before returning to his British television show, *Dr. Who*. He wasn't mean and didn't ignore me, he just wasn't bothered to get to know me. His knotted hand clasped a glass of wine and a tobacco pipe sat next to him. He had a trimmed white beard, and closely cropped white hair parted far back on his head. I thought he looked like Jacques Cousteau when he wore his stocking cap.

When I got up to use the bathroom in the night grandpa was walking around the house naked. He was hunched over with a big lump forming on his back between his shoulders, and his butt cheeks sagged down.

He puttered around in the dark moving in between the shapes of furniture. I thought he was lost.

"Hi there young man," he said. He poured a glass of water and his gnarled fingers gripped it and shook as he moved through the house lifting up a book and setting it back down. He found his pipe and returned to his room.

"I saw grandpa walking around naked last night," I said to Grandma the next morning.

"Oh, yes," she said. "He's a nudist. Always enjoyed going to naked colonies." I didn't know what was weirder, the fact that my grandma and grandpa lived in separate rooms, their strange accents or that my grandpa walked naked around the house. I looked at grandpa now in his khaki shorts, legs crossed, watching another British show, and chuckling to himself. I couldn't get his saggy butt out of my head (I still can't). He took a biscotti cookie between his thumb and middle finger and worked his teeth around it.

"Is grandpa Jewish?"

"No, he's from a Catholic family from Wimbledon."

"Did grandpa fight in World War II?"

"No, he was a conscientious objector, a pacifist. They made him serve on hospital ships out of Singapore. Your mom and grandpa were very close, my sweet," grandma said with a slight, apologizing smile. "He's old and sick now, but he cares about you." The kettle started whistling.

"Do you think my mom is in heaven?" I asked grandma. I assumed I knew her answer. Of course she did. She set a cup of tea down in front of me, and I dipped a sugar cube in the hot beverage watching it soak up the liquid before licking it.

"No, my dear."

"You don't believe she is in heaven?" I said. I was shocked at the response and felt my lip quiver. "Why? What did she do? Why wouldn't she be in heaven?"

"I don't believe in that stuff."

Tightness formed in my chest and tears welled up in my eyes. I wiped them before they ran down my cheeks. I refused to listen to her anymore. I got up from the table and ran to my room crawling under the bed. I wanted nothing to do with her. I saw her white leather nurse shoes, and felt the bed flex over me as she sat.

"It's only this old, haggard woman's opinion," she said. "Don't listen to this old biddy. Please forgive me." She sat for a while not saying anything. My feet hung out the side of the bed frame. "Do you believe she is in heaven?"

"Yes," I said.

"Then that's all that matters, my boy. It doesn't matter what I say."

"Where do you think she is?" There was only silence.

"Gone."

There was a sting in that word. My mom was her daughter, so I didn't understand how she didn't want to believe she was near, or in a better place. How could she not want my mother's soul to be near? It was as if her very denial robbed me of the one comfort I clung to. My mom was in heaven watching over me.

"It's a terrible thing to live longer than your child," she said rocking on the bed above me. "She died way too young."

I didn't answer her until the bed creaked relieving the pressure above me and her feet slipped out the door. I lay under that bed praying to escape it all. I stared at the fibers in the wool carpet. She came back to check on me. Minutes turned to hours.

"How are you, my sweets?" grandma said.

"Did you love my mom?" I uttered hours later.

"Of course I did."

"How do you know?"

"I just do."

"You just do. Well, I know she watches over me. I just do."

"Aaron, you can believe that, it's okay." But it was as if her absence of belief diminished my own, and my mom's spirit.

"Don't you like to think my mom's nearby?" I asked.

"It's a nice thought, yes. So come out from under the bed." She patted my leg, which stuck out from under the frame. "Your mother loved books, Aaron. Why don't we go to the library and find you some books? Nothing like a good book to get your mind off bad things."

I realized I never knew what mom liked to read. Or her favorite food, or what music she listened to. There was so much I didn't know about her and probably never would. "What did my mom like to read?"

"Oh, she read everything. She started reading before she ever went to school. She loved poems. What do you like to read?"

"I don't know."

"Come on *boychick*, we can figure it out."

"Why don't you believe in God?" I said from underneath the bed.

"Many reasons. I guess it started in the bathroom when I was a child, a little older than you."

16

Wait the big downpour out in a cave.

Belgium

The train of refugees spent days crisscrossing Belgium and its hedgerows and rolling green fields. Bags billowed out like the stuffing from an old coat. Men and children poked their heads through windows for brief freedom, and women hung shirts and pants.

Letty noticed details of the car, the grains in its wood and the lines in the elders' faces around her. She recognized some of these faces from their neighborhood. Through the stacks of suitcases and refugees she saw the rabbi from father's synagogue. It was the rabbi that spoke to her on the street when she was a child waiting for Gentiles to turn off their lights. Observant Jews can't use electricity after sundown on Friday, so someone had to be found to flip the switch, which was Letty's chore. He had commended her on doing a "good duty", and now he was consoling a family. Their eyes looked at him for answers and reassurance.

None knew that right behind them the Belgian Army was being routed by the Germans, as were the French and British armies. The Germans invaded France through the Ardennes forests—where no one thought to protect—driving their tanks right around the heavily fortified Maginot line that ended at the forest like an unfinished, useless fence. German Panzer tank divisions sliced through the allied armies.

Just south from where their neighbor Mrs. Weiner's family was cut down by the German gunboat, the entire British Army of more than 330,000 soldiers abandoned their armored vehicles on the beach at Dunkirk and climbed aboard thousands of English fishing boats and trawlers to escape. British citizens pulled their soldiers aboard, rescuing the entire Royal Army from the Germans.

Soon the fleeing Belgian Army caught up to their train. A locomotive pulling cars loaded with Belgian soldiers and cannons came along parallel to their train, its men smoking cigarettes in passive calmness that comes with admitting defeat. They made no expressions and stared into the distance, the wind blowing the dust from their hair and uniforms. The train passed by and its track diverted the men southwest, but then there was another train, the same as the last, next to them filled with more retreating soldiers.

All heard the buzz of German Stuka dive-bombers above. They were close. Letty cranked her neck to see them, but only saw blue sky. Then the machine gun fire rose above all other noise as German fighters strafed their train. She dove to the floor and the Stukas made pass after pass, the bullets raining down and hitting the railway cars. She was safe from bullets at the bottom of the pile crammed between benches and bodies, but had to fight for breathing space by squirming through the squeezing bodies that were like a boa constrictor.

The Belgian soldiers on the other train returned fire and the firefight seemed to last an eternity as the Stukas harassed them like buzzing mosquitoes. Children cried and mother was mumbling Hebrew words. Suzy's rough elbows swung back and forth creating space as she dug to the bottom of the heap.

Their train car dimmed and became pitch black and the gunfire stopped, the train slowed to a standstill. It was silent except for the human noises of coughing, sniveling, and whispering, and some nervous chatter.

"Is it safe?" someone said. When they unfurled themselves from the floor the blackness outside of the train, darker than night, was startling. Only the faint lights of the train car helped Letty see. Perhaps it was luck or maybe skill, but the train driver navigated into a tunnel shielding them from the diving Stukas. He stopped in the middle to force the flying beasts to find another target.

Mother gathered herself, adjusting her *sheitel* and Annie grabbed her arms and slowly climbed off the train with the rest of the shell-shocked passengers. Matches and the soft light from the train cars illuminated the tunnel enough to see the faint glow of moving silhouettes up and down the track. They huddled in the musty railway tunnel and heard deep howling of grief echoing in the shaft. There were no injuries in their car, but the wails told Letty others weren't so lucky.

The rabbi broke into a sermon. His beard glistened in the flickering glow of a burning match. Refugees gravitated towards him along the track. When one match burned to the fingers another was lit.

"Man is born to toil," he said as he squinted to see the obscure faces around him. "When the Israelites marched exultantly out of Egypt to Sinai they were a nation of miracles and invincible to the world. But the audacious nomadic tribe, the Amalekites, attacked them unprovoked and repeatedly. We are commanded to remember the Amalek. Their memory is the ever-present reminder that there will always be obstacles and deterrents that a Jew confronts in his reflection of the Torah. We have the power to overcome all such 'Amalekites.' We stand in this tunnel facing obstacles as Jews, and we will emerge from it in the light of day with resolve to meet the challenges that stand in our way. There is no Amalek of any kind that is a match for the divine power of your Jewish soul."

Shivers ran up Letty's spine at the edge of the track as his voice rose and shook reverberating through the cramped tunnel's dripping walls of cement, wood, and earth. Mother's focus was intense, squeezing Suzy's arm. Yet, Letty didn't see how God's "obstacles" helped those grieving on this track for their dead loved ones.

Yells along the railroad echoed in French to get on the train or be left behind!

Letty's stomach growled. Food was all she thought about. Suzy had biscuits in her pocket given to her by another passenger and she nibbled them when she thought no one was looking. It made Letty hungrier watching her. She became obsessed with Suzy's hands waiting for her to grab a piece of biscuit. Seeing how long Suzy could make her biscuit last was how she passed the hours. Letty could make a little piece of chocolate last a week. When the rattle and rocking of the train coaxed her mind away from the hunger and thirst a distant bomb would remind her of the diving German planes and then her hunger again. She no longer smelled the odors of the overflowing toilet, or saw the stains of excrement and grease on her dress. The lipstick and powder on her face was smeared and rubbed off. Food was all that mattered.

The train slowed and stopped in a village, its white farmhouses rising from the fields of green grass. Men and children stuck their heads out the windows and into the late spring air. Villagers stared up at them.

"Food!" the children yelled. "Food!" Letty's knees buckled and tears formed in her eyes.

Refugees pushed to get to the door first. Hunger dominated everyone's thoughts. Letty was stuck in the middle of the train and impatience pressed all around. It was a stark new reality; food was limited.

Suzy stepped around a family standing in her way and worked her way to another family at the front of the meal line. Annie and Letty stayed with mother packed in the back of the train. Letty watched through the train window as Suzy was served potatoes, cabbage and bread. It was another half-hour before Letty wound her way through the line to the pots of leftovers and brought mother some food.

"Here you go," she said. Mother pushed it away. "You need to eat. This may be the last meal for days—"

"Don't tell me what I need to do," mother said. "Do you know how this was prepared? Is it Kosher?" Letty shook her head, no. "Then I will not eat. You shouldn't either, but I'm not going to stop you. So eat."

"Do you feel alright?" Annie said and she shaded her with her body.

"How can I feel alright?" mother said throwing her hand up. "Look at where we are. Look! Nothing but dumb questions from you. Where's Suzy?" Mother swiveled her head around the crowd of refugees seeing Suzy talking to a family near the train door. Mother rested back knowing her oldest was near.

17

Stand up for your friends.

French Border

France hadn't yet collapsed under Germany and many believed they would hold out against them as they had done during World War I. The roads were clogged with refugees on foot and in cars with mattresses and chairs tied on top. Trucks were loaded with families on the roofs swaying with the road. There were carts being pulled by man and beast and still more walking along the roads coming from every direction as refugees flowed in from the small paths and the veins of the countryside pumping into the main arterial roads that fed toward the French border. With the sheer number of refugees, over four million, on the motorways the French Army found it impossible to move their troops to reinforce battle lines. German Stuka dive-bombers turned their guns on the refugees, strafing clogged lanes sowing panic and chaos along the border.

Letty's train was stopped in a long line of locomotives hauling loads of people for as far as her eyes could see. She sat there with her thoughts going over all the different outcomes. "What if they don't let us through? What do we do then? Will mother be okay?" She looked at the little bag hanging around her neck mother had sown for her passport. Was this enough to let them through?

The French tightened the borders checking for spies and saboteurs among the refugees. The train rolled a few inches and just as it started moving, it stopped, and they were stuck again with their meandering thoughts. It went like that for hours sitting in the stuffy train car made hotter by all of the angst.

"We must find God in the details of each moment," the rabbi said over the hum of the frightened car. He stood trying to relax the tension. "Passover reminds us every year that God can be wherever God chooses to be, even in the simple act of eating a piece of *matzah*. Sitting here we must find God in the difficult and tedious."

They got closer to the checkpoint and in an instant French police wearing cylinder hats, blue coats, tall boots and sporting mustachios walked along the train examining and pointing their fingers. Letty was excited because it meant their train might move. Others were more apprehensive.

In the distance French officials stood, in fancy suits, under a makeshift canopy taking stock of the refugee crisis on their border. They nodded heads at the "refugee trains" and ordered the police to move on Letty's with a flick of their fingers.

A group of policemen entered near the engine and then others on the outside started barring the doors so no one could leave. Letty looked around at other passengers trying to comprehend what was going on. The police were methodically going from car to car checking for infiltrators. They began yelling at the travelers in French to present their identification.

"*Passeports maintenant!*"

People like Blima who didn't understand French were confused by the assertive tones and direction. It didn't matter.

"*Vous m'avez entendu? J'ai dit, 'Passeports maintenant!'*" a policeman yelled at mother. Letty translated to her that he wanted her passport.

Mother grabbed her little bag around her neck. She didn't want to offend him as she fumbled for her papers, but her little bags came in handy. Others rifled through their bundles of clothes looking for documents to prove they weren't up to trouble. Their bewildered looks only antagonized the police, who were overwhelmed by the sheer amount of foreign people flooding into their country.

Police grabbed at the toothless old man next to mother showing him he needed paperwork and pointed at Blima's paperwork to show him what he needed.

"They need your papers," Letty said to the man in Yiddish.

The old man put his hands out pleading to the policeman that he meant no harm, but he was unable to find his papers in the bag. They must have been lost on the journey. He dug again and shook his head.

"He can't find them," Letty said in French to the tall policeman who was so young he only had fuzz on his lip. "Please let him in. He means no harm. He's just an old man."

The volume of voices rose and children cried. The hours of waiting were blowing up into full-fledged panic, as many feared they were going to be dragged off.

The train sighed and steam spewed into the air. They were about to move. Sensing the mood the rabbi stood up and started reciting verses from the Torah to calm the passengers. He was speaking in Hebrew, the common language of everyone on the train, except the policemen.

Letty didn't even hear the rabbi's words over the rising hysteria around her. Her sisters stayed quiet and mother stared at her daughters to translate what was going on. The young policeman, seeing the rabbi speaking to the people yelled to him to be quiet. *"Ta gueule!"*

The rabbi went silent and had a puzzled look on his face. Before anyone said anything the policemen charged at him fearing he was signaling enemies on the train. They pushed people aside to get at the rabbi, his greying beard getting caught in the police's hands as they grabbed his chest and dragged him over the bags and bodies in the aisle.

"Vous venez avec nous!" the policeman said dragging him towards the door.

"I'm only trying to help you," the rabbi said in Yiddish, trying to plead with them. But his harsh, foreign words only strengthened their purpose. Everyone was paralyzed with inaction as the rabbi was hauled out like a criminal and arrested. Something came over Letty in that split moment.

"Stop!" she yelled. No one was speaking up for the rabbi. So Letty did. Without thinking she yelled again at the police, "Stop!"

The train of speechless refugees swung their heads at the girl with the gall to challenge authority. All eyes were on her and she felt the air suck out from the train car. "Uh oh," she thought realizing she didn't think this out, but it was too late. The policemen were now staring at her.

"He means no harm," she said in French. "He's innocent. I've known him since I was a girl."

The policemen stared at each other. Perhaps she was the one he was signaling?

"Well you come along too!" an older policeman said.

In an instant, police grabbed her arms, their strong grips pressing into her flesh. She was pulled up above the floor. People stared, the whites of the their eyes enlarged, as Letty's shoe's dragged over bags and people as she was hoisted off the train. The refugees were too afraid to do anything that might earn them the same fate.

"No!" Letty heard mother screech as they removed her off the train. Blima went into a hysteric fit of screaming and crying seeing her daughter taken. The train was about to leave without her youngest. She pushed Suzy up.

"Get your sister back!" she said. "Do what you have to. Get her back!"

Suzy looked at mother's face and then pushed passed the silent refugees to the door. There was no time to waste as the train sighed again. A policeman stood blocking her way. She smiled at him.

"Please officer, let me get my sister," she said. He shook his head not moving from the door. "She doesn't know what she's done. I'll talk sense into her. And make sure she's not a headache for you. Please, she's young."

I don't know if it was what she said, but he stepped aside. Refugees stuck their heads out the windows watching like spectators. Suzy jumped down the stairs and saw Letty being pulled along the tracks toward a canopy filled with men in suits.

Suzy came running from behind in pursuit. Before the police had a chance to say anything to her, she wound her arm back and gave Letty a huge wallop on the behind and kept beating her as hard she could until tears ran down Letty's cheeks. In the background the train's whistle blew letting everyone know it was about to leave.

"What are you doing, girl?" the policeman said. He was surprised by her sudden arrival as he was by her fury. Letty's body throbbed, but it caused the policeman pause.

"Officer, this is my sister," she said. "She is only a child and acts without thought. She didn't mean to offend you. She is just a dumb girl. Please let her back on the train and we'll punish her for this disrespect."

He looked at Suzy for a moment studying her face trying to judge the merits of her words. He then glanced over to the group of officials now watching the scene. One of the men motioned to the identification around Letty's neck. The policeman took her ID card out and studied the picture glancing at it and then at Letty all the while still holding her arm with a firm grip.

"Officer—," Letty said.

"Not a word out of you," he said. "What's her name?" he said to Suzy studying Letty's information and her face. The train blew its whistle again, and Letty stared up the track and saw the train engineers climbing up the locomotive. Letty turned her head back to her sister.

Suzy was about to blurt out "Letty," but stopped just as the "L" formed on her tongue. Letty's heart leaped in her chest and her breath stopped for a moment. Her nickname was always Letty since she was a small girl, but it wasn't her given name that was on the paperwork.

"Zlata Schmidt from Antwerp, Belgium," Suzy said. Letty's breathing started again. Her cousin Hanka started calling her "Letty" when

62

they were children, and it stuck.

"Let me see your ID," he said pointing to the bag around Suzy's neck. She handed it over. The train's brakes released with a steam hiss and it was ready to roll toward France.

He compared the IDs by holding them next to each other. With the officials watching him, he wasn't going to make a mistake. When he was satisfied he nodded his boyish face at the officials observing from under the shade of the canopy. The one that seemed to be in charge gave a simple nod of his head toward the train and the policeman let go his grip of Letty's arm.

The train lurched forward and people on the train yelled at them, "Hurry!" Suzy dug her nails deep into her little sister's arm and they ran back toward the train car. She didn't let her grip go even as they jumped over train tracks. Letty peered over her shoulder at the rabbi who was pulled by a policeman toward the group of officials. He looked back at her and there was a smile. She didn't know if it was fear on his face, or confusion, or if he was just happy that somebody stood up for him.

They jumped on the moving train and she watched from its steps as police led the rabbi off in the other direction toward a line of trucks. Men with dogs walked up and down the tracks. The rabbi disappeared in the smoke and steam of the train. Letty turned and went inside, grateful for Suzy's intervention.

"Stupid girl!" mother said and struck Letty hard across the face. Minutes later the train crossed into France.

18

If it seems too good to be true, it probably is.

Luchon, France

While most of Europe was coming unraveled, Letty's train wound its way to the small resort town just north of the Spanish border, Bagnères de Luchon, high in the Pyrenees. At the end of the eight-day trip from Antwerp, which should have lasted one, mountain peaks piercing a deep blue sky surrounded them.

With stunning beauty, grand hotels and bathhouses all around, the refugees were herded off the train car in Luchon and funneled into a circular building where straw was thrown on the floor. Letty looked at the faces and families huddled on the floor. They were all Jews. Local police were posted outside the door to guard them.

"This is not acceptable!" a man said to a guard. He was dressed in a suit, now soiled and stained from the trip. "I'm a lawyer. I'll file a petition of inhumane living standards with the UN and Red Cross!"

The way he said it scared the policeman. It wasn't long before a city official, short and balding, walked into the hall and looked the haggard travelers over. He huddled in a corner with the refugee lawyer, who pointed at the hay and then to Letty's sisters. The city official threw his hands in the air and stormed off resisting the lawyer's arguments.

"I can't take much more of this," mother said. "Look at us. Filthy as pigs in hay." She pushed herself up and paced around the building and found a group of women from her neighborhood in Antwerp willing to hear her complaints.

After a day sleeping on the floor the mayor relented and moved the Jewish refugees to the Hotel Sacarron, where the King of Belgium himself had once stayed. Letty flopped down feeling the squish and softness wrap around her body of the bed. It was the first time she felt comfortable in two weeks.

Mother went to close the door of the room, but there was no lock. She looked at the door on the old building trying to find a latch. She noticed thin cracks in the wall and saw a person's eye on the other side.

"Oh, there is someone staring at us!" she screamed in a shrill and incredulous pitch. Letty and her sisters got up to see, but there was no eye, only the empty crack for prying eyes. Letty stuffed a sock in the wall and tried securing the door. Nothing they tried kept the door locked.

There was a beat of a drum and a man yelled from the street, "Listen here! Listen here! The mayor of Luchon says that all Jews must present themselves to city hall." When Letty ran to the window to see the man he was gone.

"What did he say?" mother asked, not understanding French.

"Jews must go to city hall," Letty said.

"We must go," mother said. "They will throw us out of the city or arrest us if we don't."

There were crowds of Jewish refugees scared to disobey the order waiting in silence at City Hall. Officials and police moved around the refugees. Letty and her family were ushered into a line where the bald official from days earlier studied their passports and wrote down their names, recorded that they were Jewish, and gave them ration books and identity cards. Now their Jewishness was on record.

As they walked back to their room, on Letty's arms she noticed pus-filled boils and sores. She looked at her legs. They were all over her calves too.

"Oh, no. Suzy, look," Letty said. "What is this?"

Mother examined her arms and wiped her forehead. The sores were oozing on Letty's leg.

"What did you go and do?" she said.

"Nothing," Letty said.

"Look, Suzy has one on her neck," Annie said pointing it out. Suzy reached up flinching as she ran her fingers over it. Letty then saw Annie had one on her arm.

"Annie, you have one there," Letty said.

They checked mother. She had them all over her legs and arms. The sores must have popped up over night. Was it dirt? Disease? Infection? A woman from their old neighborhood in Antwerp said it was from filth and their soiled clothes, so the family scrubbed them in a washbasin.

The boils itched, dripped puss and stung with each scratch. Letty wrapped her body before she left the hotel feeling the shame of the little boils. They were on display for all to see and she didn't know how to get rid of them.

It was the group of women from Antwerp with whom mother spent her days gossiping who said that the mayor of Luchon had a plan to "help" the Jewish refugees. They were picking his hillsides for every last bit of food and turned his picturesque resort town into a disease-infested squalor. Annie, Suzy and Letty did forage for anything that looked edible along with the thousands of other refugees. Letty found carrots in one field and Annie a potato in another, and there was an egg near an old farm. Mother fixed the food in the chimney of their new living quarters in the Saccron hotel.

The mayor circulated news to the refugees of "a great opportunity to emigrate to Spain" and that he would issue travel visas.

"Letty, find out about this Spanish visa," mother said. "The women say it's a good chance for us." She sent Annie out too. Suzy was nowhere to be found.

Letty left the front door of the hotel and there was a boy with floppy dark hair kicking a rubber ball against the wall. She had seen him before and he was probably about her age. Another boy with black hair ran over to him, and they caromed the ball off the wall so that it went in wild directions.

"Are you going to get a visa to Spain?" Letty asked. The boy with floppy hair stopped the small rubber ball with his foot and pushed his hair from his face. His brown eyes surveyed her. The thin mountain air made Letty breathe fast and the morning sun that crept down the side of the building made her look down at her feet.

"My father says it's just a trick," he said. His friend stood near, but didn't say anything.

"What do you mean?" she said.

"He's trying to clear us out," the boy said.

"How does your father know?" Letty wanted to make sure the boy wasn't trying to fool her.

"He's a lawyer. What's your name?"

"Letty. What's yours?"

"Theo, and that's Daniel," he said pointing to other boy. "Don't waste your time trying to get those visas. How old are you?"

"I'm going to be seventeen. You?"

"I'm seventeen," he said. He spoke French in an accent she knew was from Belgium. He continued to kick his ball against the wall, the stone edges shooting it catawampus. His quick feet trapped the ball like a cat at the last second. "Do you want to kick it too?"

"Sure." The ball shot off the wall and she blocked it with her feet.

"Kick it!" Letty flipped it with her toe and it hopped touching the wall and stopped. "No, like this." Theo banged it with his foot and it flew at the wall.

By the time Letty returned mother was almost convinced by the women to take the mayor up on his offer. "This could be a good opportunity," she said.

"But the mayor doesn't have the authority to grant travel visas to

Spain," Annie said. "It's a trick." Annie heard the same information as Letty and was trying to convince mother that Spain wasn't an option, only a waste of time.

"Are you sure?" mother said. Annie nodded, yes.

The next day Letty watched refugees gather their possessions and walk out the hotel toward the Spanish border, about a 15-minute drive from Luchon, but it was at least a two-hour walk. Many hitchhiked and some went by foot all day to the Spanish border. The mayor had given them exit visas for Spain. The Schmidts stayed put.

19

There can be beauty amidst the bombs.

The French army fought the Germans for another month putting up stiff resistance, but Hitler's Luftwaffe air force and Panzer tank divisions outflanked the remaining French forces. When resistance collapsed, control of France was carved up. The Nazis occupied the north and west zone of France, Italy controlled a zone in the southeast and the French Vichy government ruled the "unoccupied zone," the *zone libre.* It was in the Vichy zone where Luchon fell on the map. Marshal Philippe Pétain, a French national hero from World War I, became France's leader, and Pétain was quick to be a compliant partner with Hitler.

Philippe Pétain meeting Hitler in 1940.

Blima had registered for immigration to the United States and told her daughters they had distant relatives in Providence, RI who were "well-off." If they could get out of France they would be "taken care of." Letty always assumed this family, the Hassenfelds, were somewhat wealthy, but she didn't know they were the owners of a major American toy business: The Hassenfeld Brothers would eventually become Hasbro Inc., one of the largest toy companies in the world, the name originating from the "Hassenfeld Brothers." But getting out of France would be a challenge.

Near the foyer of the hotel Theo sat in the morning sun—his eyes closed, a book in his lap. When he saw Letty he got up, pushing his hair from his eyes, and slid the book into his back pocket. His calm stroll said he belonged in this mountain retreat.

He had been right about the mayor of Luchon making things up. When the refugees arrived at the Spanish checkpoint puzzled border patrol guards refused them entry. They said the stamp in their passports was worthless and the mayor had no authority to grant visas to their country. Over the day people trickled back lugging their things, and an angry mob formed outside the mayor's office.

"Did you get a visa?" Theo said.

"You were right," Letty said.

"I hope you didn't walk all the way to Spain?"

"No, you saved us a trip. Though I hear the countryside is beautiful."

"You want to see it now?"

"What do you mean?"

"C'mon. Hike with me through the country."

"I need to find food. My mother is waiting."

"You said you wanted to see the country. Plus you have to find food. I know where to find eggs. Even oranges."

Letty knew mother's position on going out with boys alone; it was strictly forbidden.

"Which way are you going?" she said. Theo pointed towards the mountain peaks in the distance. She didn't say anything, but started

70

walking in that direction.

She walked with Theo through the town and by the shops. The war seemed a million miles away as he pointed to cakes in a window. When they reached the end of the main street they kept walking. Soon fields with only a lone farmhouse on the hill were all that was around. A few nervous glances were exchanged. Stone mountainsides broke through the ground reaching for the sky forming breathtaking vistas in the distance and they meandered through grassy meadows and under trees. They jumped over clear streams and only the sun watched. There was a sign for "*Superbagneres.*"

"I've heard of a beautiful crystal clear lake with a waterfall nearby," Theo said. "We should go."

"When?" Letty asked.

"Now."

"Now?"

"Why not?"

It was all a whim and she started stepping through the tall grass as if saying nothing was actually better than saying, "yes." Of course it wasn't, but Letty forgot these moral questions as the thin, cool air flooded her lungs and she breathed deeper and harder.

A small car bumped up the road and Theo ran towards it putting his thumb up before Letty was able to question what he was doing. The car pulled over and she heard Theo ask about the lake.

"I can take you near the trail," the driver said. Letty didn't know what she was getting herself into, and there were butterflies in her belly. The two of them jumped into the back like stowaways. It was the first time she ever hitchhiked.

The tree lined road snaked through mountain valleys with stone farmhouses and pastures. With wind blowing their hair, Theo and Letty sat in quiet content, staring out the windows at the lush, green rolling hills and creeks. About a half-hour later the driver pulled off the road near a farm and pointed to where they needed to walk.

"*Merci,*" Theo said.

It was a long hike ahead and Letty didn't know what she was going to tell her mother about why she was so late getting back. She better have found something good to eat. Those thoughts melted away as she started up the trail with this boy she just met and the muscles in her legs tightening.

The slight burn in her chest brought her gaze up from the steep gravel trail to the summer peaks and the snow still clinging in the shady crags of rock. They were two little specs in a range of pointed rock formations that went on for as far as she could see.

Theo breathed hard behind her and Blima crept back into her mind. They reached the top of the trail and looked down into a crater in the earth protected by walls of limestone and green vegetation. At the very bottom was a deep blue glass lake ringed by emerald meadows, patches of snow and at the far end a large waterfall. She stood next to Theo with hands on her hips looking into the depths of a world unknown to her. They left the madness of their lives behind, and began their decent down the siltstone footpath and their shoes skidded over the lose rocks and tufts of grass.

When they reached the edges of the crystal clear lake and smelled the pureness of air, Theo kicked off his shoes and pulled his shirt over his head and ran diving into the water. His yelps echoed off the walls of the mountains and into far-off valleys. Letty put her feet in the lake, which captured snowmelt, and it numbed her toes.

"You have to come in, Letty!" Theo swung his arms beckoning Letty to swim out to him.

It was freezing and she had pus-filled boils covering her entire body, but she also didn't know how to swim.

"Come on!" He yelled and splashed as he swam out towards the center of the blueness. "It's amazing!"

Letty watched his arms glide through the water, and his hair stand up. She wished to know how to swim more than anything in the world.

Still in her dress she ran diving into the water, but staying close to the shore like a small child. The cold encased her body penetrating the skin. It hurt and felt great. The little sores all over her body numbed in the ice water. Letty's screams bounced around the mountains and she went as far as her waist, dunking herself as if it were a baptism. Theo swam far out into the lake. The waterfall was in front of her and the peaks surrounded her and for a brief moment it was a perfect world. He glided across the small lake toward the waterfall. If she knew how to swim she would be next to him.

He bobbed under the water pushing his hair back and came back to shore dripping. They lay in a grassy field to dry off in the warm sun and she felt the buzz and tingles of the ice water. Letty tried to hide her goose bumps and boils pulling her wet dress over her legs, and concealing her arms under her sweater.

"Those sores are probably from not getting enough nutrients," Theo said without looking at her. "You're not eating enough."

"My mother and sisters have them too."

"I know others that have them," he said. "It's from malnutrition."

"You don't have any." She peered at his arms and stomach and looked away feeling hot redness in her cheeks.

"That's because I've found ways to get a little extra," Theo said with his eyes still sealed in the sun. "The rations they give won't keep you alive."

After drying they hiked over to the waterfall on the other side of the lake. Its cool mist sprayed the plants, rocks and them. Letty noticed the tattered paperback book in Theo's back pocket.

"What are you reading?"

"*Candide*," he said. "Have you read it?"

"No. What's it about?"

"A hopeless optimist," he said. She strained to hear him over the splash of the waterfall. "It's one of the only things I took with me when I fled Brussels, besides a few clothes."

They perched themselves on a ledge next to the waterfall noticing other streams running down the sides of mountains filling the lake with fresh snowmelt.

"Why did you bring that book?" Letty asked. He looked at the rushing water through his brown bangs.

"I don't know. I like the story. It reminds me to laugh at the ridiculousness. Our lives might be futile, but even if I'm disfigured and unrecognizable, I can still grow a garden and eat."

Letty listened and forgot that she was staring at him. He asked her something snapping her back to the moment. "What did you bring from Antwerp?"

"Oh, we brought an alarm clock. I don't know what my mother was thinking," Letty said. "Now my sister lugs it in her bag."

"It's weird what our parents decided to bring. We'll never see any of that stuff we left behind again. But those little things that made it in our bags become important."

It was the first time Letty thought of mother since they set foot by the lake. "I need to get back."

He put his hand out. It was damp from the waterfall's mist, but his grip was solid pulling her up from the rock. They climbed down through the crevices and boulders and back to the shore of the lake. Before she knew it they were already at the summit looking back down at the crystal blue reflections in the lake. She closed her eyes for a moment to feel the sun bake her face, and to capture the moment in her mind. They still needed to hitchhike back to Luchon, but part of her looked forward to it. Returning to mother's questions and penetrating stare was an entirely different thing.

20

Keep your feet moving.

Toulouse, France

Suzy found a boyfriend from the defeated Belgian army and through his connections she was getting extra rations, fruit, and even chocolate. She came into their room quiet and unloaded her pockets. Out of the corner of Letty's eye, she watched her put the food in her suitcase before she thought anyone noticed. She dropped the food in and covered it with her clothes and then secured the suitcase with the lock she brought from Antwerp.

"Suzy, is that chocolate?" Letty said, seeing her put it in her suitcase. Candy was hard to come by. Mother looked up from the dress she was mending.

"What are you talking about?" Suzy said.

"The chocolate you keep locked in your suitcase."

"Your boils are clearing up, Letty," Suzy said. "Seems like you've eaten your fair share. I've been wondering where you're getting extra food. Maybe mother would like to know too. Is it from that boy you've been spending time with?"

"What is Suzy talking about, Letty?" mother said.

"A boy that gave me information about Spanish visas, and gave us oranges. Remember those oranges?"

"I don't want to hear any more about him," mother said. "You are going with Annie to Toulouse. Not another word from you tonight."

Mother handed Suzy a bowl of the broth with vegetables she made over a hot fire, and when no one was looking Suzy slipped the chocolate out of her suitcase into her sweater pocket. Her suitcase lay opened and unlocked, so all could see she was hiding nothing. Without saying a word Suzy left to meet the soldier, a non-Jew from Brussels.

Before the sun broke over the eastern mountains in the morning Annie and Letty walked along the rutted road towards Toulouse. Travel restrictions prevented refugees from leaving Luchon, but if they slipped out of town in early morning to the highway it wasn't hard to leave. In the back of Letty's mind was a rumor circulating through the Jewish grapevine about an impending law to arrest foreign Jews. "Jewish lists" were being compiled throughout the French provinces through the ration books issued to refugees.

In Toulouse was the Portuguese consulate. Immigrating to Portugal would mean a few days to cross Spain, versus spending weeks crossing the Atlantic amid German U-boats and all the other ordeals of a sea voyage. Also, Annie was looking for someone.

At the road cars whipped by and they stuck their thumbs up into the cool, dawn air. A beat-up, red Peugeot truck with a tarp-covered flatbed slowed. Inside were an old farmer and his wife. Letty and Annie rode in the back as the narrow boulevards wound through rows of red tiled brick buildings and the arching bridges and markets of Toulouse. Letty pulled her hair back with a scarf and stuck her head out the flap to take in the afternoon sun's magical glow on the rusted iron and masonry.

A small crowd of people gathered and they noticed it was for the embassy. People stood agitated and kicking about, sweaty and tired when they walked up to the building.

"We're trying to get a visa for Portugal," Annie said to an old man in a shirt with sweat stains down his chest and under his pits.

"We're all here for visas," he said in Yiddish. "I've waited two days and still I haven't got to the front." The crowd of people were Jewish refugees from across Europe; men, women, children and babies all lingering to get a piece of paper in their passports that might allow them to escape. If the *gendarmes* wanted to round up foreign Jews today, this was a good spot. Languages from across Europe were spoken. Men with long *peyos* curling down their ears, beards, and hats mingled in the heat. Women and children huddled under trees and any spare bit of shade.

"It's disorder here," he said. "You don't know why some people get in and others like me stand for days. People get special treatment." He threw his hand up in the air in disgust. It didn't look promising.

The sun was hot and many passed the time sifting through the newspapers filled with pages of advertisements of families searching for each other: "Father looking for 10 year-old daughter. Disappeared on the road between Montauban and Toulouse..." "Reward for information about the location of my mother..." "Please help me find my husband and infant child, last seen in Antwerp train station May 13th..." Letty skimmed the ads looking for Bernard. Father? There wasn't much chance of that. There were hundreds here, and millions more across France stewing in silence and anxiety, waiting for news of loved ones, of visa applications, of where to go next, of threatening Vichy French decrees.

Already the Vichy authorities banned Jews from holding elected office or from serving in the military, news media, banking, and teaching, or any position that might exercise "cultural influence."

Every so often the embassy door opened and refugees' faces perked up from the newspapers as hope colored their thoughts. A few people were waved inside and a murmur rose up about how some people were chosen for entry and others not. Some more visibly upset than others crumpled their newspapers trying to hide their frustration, but not attract attention. Then papers were unwrinkled and their heads slumped over as necks reddened in the sun. This went on through the day as hundreds of refugees stood in haphazard lines that snaked to nowhere. Some changed line positions, but for no reason. Letty didn't even think about what awaited them on the other side of the door and the even slimmer chances of walking out with a visa to Portugal. For now, getting inside was all there was.

Annie turned to Letty, her face red from the sun and heat, her lips dry. "I don't think we're going to get in," she said. "Not today, at least."

When they stepped out of line people moved to take their place just as the door opened and a man in a neat tie poked his head out. He pointed his finger and several refugees, including the man they spoke to earlier, jumped up, gathered their things and shuffled up the stone steps and through the door before the official changed his mind. Letty threw her hand up without thinking trying to get the official's attention. The door closed.

It opened again moments later, and the same consulate official closed and padlocked an iron gate. "Please let us in," refugees said to the official. "We have a sick child." But the consulate wasn't letting in any more people for the day.

The crowd grew smaller as Letty and Annie walked back down towards the river by the *Capitole* and its expansive inlaid arcade and then through the rows of shops and cafes. A person in line told them of a refugee camp outside the city. "It's for men," he said. "But you can try to stay there for the night if they allow you." They had nowhere else to go.

21

Be open to finding friends in unexpected places.

There were no signs and Annie knocked on a door. It was a few buildings that looked like mechanic workshops with a large door for a car, and small door for a person next to it. The small door opened a crack, and a head pushed out.

"Is this the refugee camp?" Annie said. It was dark and the man's face was indistinguishable.

"Yes," he said.

"Do you have space for us?" she said.

"It's for men."

"Please, we have no other place to stay."

He pulled his head back in and closed the door. Letty heard him conversing with someone inside in muted whispers. One voice rose and the other subsided like a swell on the ocean. Then there was rustling and the moving of furniture.

The door creaked open.

"Come in," a voice said from inside.

"Thank you," Annie said. "We appreciate it." Letty squinted her eyes trying to see the faces of their hosts in the dim light. Annie walked in before Letty was able to grab her arm, and against better judgment, she followed inside too.

An old leather couch sat against a wall, a wood desk with a lamp and files of papers took center stage, and half the room was stuffed with hundreds of large boxes stacked to the ceiling.

"What are your names?" a petite man said. He wore a suit jacket and collared shirt buttoned to the top. He walked over to the desk and grabbed a ledger.

"Annie and Letty Schmidt," Annie said. He wrote it down, but paused a moment.

"This is a camp for men," he said. Under the small lamp Letty saw his large, skinny nose, sunken cheeks and droopy eyes. "For your protection we need to secure your door." His voice was deep and larger than his meek frame implied.

"Secure our door? Did they mean to lock us in?" Letty thought. In the corner was another man; very large and looming in the shadows near the boxes. Letty wasn't able to see his face.

"Show them to their room," the little man said. The big man set something large down behind a box. Letty heard keys jingling and he walked by them toward the door.

"Follow me," he said in a gruff whisper. She only saw his large back as they walked to a room in the building, and saw no other people. Maybe they were sleeping in another building. Her stomach was in knots, but she was too tired to be scared: It was the hunger that twisted her innards.

He opened a door and they walked into a room with two beds. It was tidy and had pictures on the wall of the Garonne River, which meandered through the center of Toulouse.

"Are you hungry?" he said.

"A little," Annie said. The husky man with hair pouring out of his shirt neck, left and returned moments later with a baguette and a piece of cured ham. Letty hadn't eaten like this since she arrived in France. He closed the door. She heard the keys jingling and the bolt in the lock fasten them in. Letty was happy to have a bed and food. This wasn't any ordinary camp with food like this.

Her ears adjusted to the environment and she listened to their hosts' whispers talking about Red Cross grain shipments and reselling them to other refugee camps "for a profit." The camp seemed a storefront for black market deals. Food was a huge commodity and farmers diverted portions of their crops to the black market where they could get the highest prices.

Annie didn't sleep either. Instead she knocked on the locked door.

"Are you crazy?" Letty said. "They are *Mafiosos*."

She ignored Letty and knocked louder.

There was a jingling of keys and the door opened. The big man stood there like a dark shadow in the doorway saying nothing.

"Sorry to bother you so late," Annie said. "Do you know how I could get in contact with my friend in another camp?"

"Which camp?"

"I don't know. That's the problem. I don't even know if she made it to France." Letty suspected Annie was talking about Toby from Behr's travel agency, Annie's best friend.

"Place an ad in the newspaper. Or write refugee camps." He was about to close the door, but stopped, inspecting the cracks in the stucco wall. "If you write to the refugee camps take care in the words you use. The Vichy read your letters."

He disappeared, but came back with a map and went over the different Jewish refugee camps in the area pointing to places Annie's friend might have gone after leaving Antwerp. At least two of the locations were where Annie already knew Toby had family near. Annie scanned the area making mental notes as the big man, speaking so soft you needed to lean in to hear him, showed the web of refugee camps throughout France.

He tried to close the door and go back to his business, but Annie stopped the door with her hand.

"We need to go to the Portuguese embassy tomorrow morning. Can you let us out early? We want the front of the line." In the back of Letty's mind she wondered if her hosts had other plans for them.

"There's a small chance they'll let you in," he said, folding his arms. "Bang on the door and I'll see you get there." His face was missing its morning shave and if you didn't look close, soft eyes were lost underneath the sharp edge of his thick eyebrows.

"Why do you say that?" Annie said.

"You need to know someone. You might get lucky. But then again, you know hitting your head against a wall hurts so you don't do it." His eyebrows relaxed and he unfolded his arms putting his hand on the doorjamb, his large body taking up most of the space.

"We risked trouble with police to come here," she said.

"Well try then," he said. "Police are increasing checks of camps. They require us to provide lists of the men that come through here. You're not men, so I'll not include your names." He looked at the map of France that was in his hand. "The U.S. embassy in Marseille is easier."

"Why?" Annie said.

"Because they have numbered tickets you take for appointment," he said. "All I have to do is write a man and he will have a number waiting for you when you arrive. You'll see an official right away. Easy as that, but once you get in, that's a different story. Not like this Portuguese embassy."

"What do I need to do for the U.S. embassy?"

"Every detail down to the dotted 'i' is important," he said. "They'll reject you for the smallest detail. If you have a sponsorship, you should be approved—"

"We do." He nodded and locked the door.

In the morning Annie tapped on the door and two minutes later keys jingled and the door was opened. The big man stood waiting.

"Here's my contact's address in Marseille. Write him with the day and he will have an appointment at the embassy waiting."

The big man dropped them near the Portuguese embassy and already mobs of people were waiting hours before the embassy opened. They stepped out into the cool morning. The crowd was growing larger than yesterday. Letty's stomach gurgled and twisted with nausea.

"Your face is white," Annie said. "Are you okay?"

22

Focus on the details.

Luchon, France

She saw the face of a man talking to her, but didn't know what he said. Was it French? She lay bouncing in the back of a car. A hand ran through her hair. Annie, where are we going?

Her hunger was gone, which was a relief. Mother now dabbed her forehead with a wet cloth. Only her head swiveled from side to side, the rest of her body was paralyzed, sapped of any energy. She watched Annie through blurry sight, whose head stared down at the small table writing and going over papers. What was she doing? Letty opened her mouth to call out, but no words came.

Mother paced by her through the small room and put her hand on her forehead. There was little to do except wait. She wanted to hike to the lake again with that boy, Theo, and read *Candide*. Her blankets and clothes draped over her exposing knobby knees, rib cage and collarbones. Mother made soup from the roots Annie brought to keep something in Letty's body. Suzy asked Annie about the U.S. visa. What visa? They didn't get the Portuguese visa. She wanted to look it over.

Mother spooned hot consommé into Letty's mouth. She vomited, not able to keep anything in her stomach.

"How could you get sick like this?" mother said. "You're always running around. What did you expect? How could you do this to me?

Letty, you are going to be the death of me."

The week was an eternity. Then one day her flaccid limbs felt blood pulsing in them again and strength returned. She felt bad they didn't get the Portuguese visa. It was her fault for getting sick.

Annie held a letter high in the room and hugged mother, whose tight lips cracked a smile. It was from the Hassenfelds. Letty still lay in bed and didn't grasp the importance. She did remember the big man and his sausage fingers poking at the map.

"It's our ticket to America," Annie said. She held the documents up in the air shaking them like a golden ticket. "It's our way out!"

One of the main criteria for getting a visa to the United States was proof of sponsorship. But for the U.S. Embassy to take a visa request seriously, the sponsor needed to have sufficient funds in the bank. When mother said the Hassenfelds were "quite well-off," Letty didn't comprehend how rich they were. Annie showed their bank statement to her sisters. There were more zeros than Letty had ever seen. She thought they were sure to get the visa, and so did mother.

It was now down to the logistics of getting to Marseille to file the application. It was a five-hour ride from Luchon and even longer when you hitchhiked. Letty was still getting her strength back, and Annie wrote letters and filled out applications from dawn to dusk.

"This is our best hope," mother said. She clung to the prospect of a life in the U.S. She didn't have the language skills or capacity to make it happen, but Annie did. Even so, she second-guessed every aspect of Annie's plan. It was a five-hour trip up the coast of France along the Mediterranean Sea into areas they had never seen and into different Vichy zones run by different governors.

"You will not contact a stranger in Marseille," mother said when Annie told her of the big man's contact. "I forbid it."

"I need to get into the embassy. It'll be days if I don't have someone take a ticket for me. I may not get in. It happened in Toulouse."

"I have a cousin in Marseille," mother said. "Contact him." Annie wrote another letter.

A couple weeks later mother's cousin wrote. Annie wasted no time throwing her things in a small bag. She studied the documents one more time making sure everything was as it should be. She ran her index finger over the requirements and then looked at all the papers that lay in front of her.

23

It's okay to "forget" your I.D. at home.

Letty didn't recall the day Annie left. When her strength returned she went foraging for food in the fields around Luchon, and to meet Theo, who she hadn't seen since she left for Toulouse two weeks earlier. Theo and Letty came to the large thermal bathhouse, Thermes de Luchon, which stood out as a beacon for all to gaze upon. Underneath the old, white manor with arcades and columns resting at the foot of the mountain was a cavern of hot springs.

"I have a surprise," Theo said. "This will help with your recovery." Theo found a side door that wasn't locked leading through a series of hallways. In the name of Letty's recovery they crept through the building hugging the walls and found an access door that staff used for cleaning. The old knob squeaked as Theo turned it and they heard footsteps coming their direction. They rushed into the dimly lit maze, bits of light catching the damp tiles on the wall as dark tunnels went in two directions. Sulphurous smells flooded Letty's senses and beads of perspiration formed on her forehead. They followed one long, narrow hall for a while keeping their voices low and their eyes scanning for people. The silence was eerie. They arrived at pools of hot water with steam rising in the low glimmer of the bulbs running alongside the wet pathway.

"Let's go for a dip," Theo said. He had a sly smile. "There's no one around. These baths have good healing qualities." Before she had time to protest, his shoes and shirt flew off and he grimaced as he went in, careful not to make too loud of a noise.

Letty put her feet in the hot water, which emitted a strong odor of rotten eggs, and at first touch it burned her toes like a scalding bath. These were thermal waters from the center of the earth. She was still weak from her illness and slid into the molten bathwater, her eyes closed in a trance. Letty's worries leached out of her pores and her heart throbbed in her ears.

When Letty could pry her eyelids open from their stupor, there was a pair of shoes and legs standing over them. She closed her eyes again thinking she was seeing something, but they were still there. Letty nudged Theo and his eyes opened.

"What are your names?" a voice asked. They didn't answer trying to grasp this person who spoke with authority. "Identification, now."

"We don't have our books," she said. "Sorry, we forgot them." It was hard for police to process them without I.D.

"You must carry your books at all times," he said. He wore a dark suit and had a trimmed mustache. "You are not permitted to be here. Let me get you some towels." His tone changed from authoritative to kind. He walked down the tunnel his steps resounding on the tile floors as he faded in the darkness.

"It's a policeman," Theo whispered and nodded his head. "Let's go."

They slipped out of the water and gathered their things and hurried down the other tunnel before the man returned. Winding their way back through they heard steps behind. "Hello? Where are you?" the policeman called out. "There's nowhere to go! Just this passageway that goes nowhere!" His voice echoed through taunting them.

They started jogging and dripped over the floor. "Where's the door?" Theo said. His clothes crumpled in his arms.

"Up here," Letty said. They ran through the humid passageway searching the tile walls. Their bare feet were quiet, but they left a trail of water drops for their pursuer.

"I'll remember your faces!" the policeman said behind them somewhere in the chamber of pools. "Especially you, boy! I've seen you before!" They heard his steps coming. "If you give yourselves up I'll let you off with a warning, but if I catch you I'm going to haul you in. It's your choice!"

They looked at each other. It wasn't much of a choice. They continued their search hoping the policeman wasn't waiting for them at the service entrance.

Up in front Theo pointed. It was the door. He put his clothes on and Letty slipped on her shoes. Her dress was soaking wet and stuck to her. The steps came closer. Theo opened the door with a delicate touch remembering the squeak, and peeked his head through. The pitter-patter of dress shoes quickened through the tunnel. His hand grabbed Letty's and pulled her through and they raced out into the old manor house, its hardwood floors creaking under their feet and portrait paintings looking down from the oak walls. Staff members in white uniforms stared as they rushed to the nearest exit. Letty tried door after door but they were locked. Then she saw an open gate and ran into the crisp mountain air.

They looked over their shoulders and jogged into the pastures and hid against a stonewall. There was a herd of grazing cows in front of them, and nothing else but fields.

"Do you think he was really a policeman, or just a bathhouse employee?" Letty said between breaths. "He was saying all that stuff to scare us."

"I think he was police," Theo said.

"Why?"

"I've seen him before," he said. "He was at our hotel with another policeman getting the names. You know they are collecting information on all the refugees?"

"We could leave Luchon," Letty said. "Go to Toulouse. Or Spain, Portugal."

"It would be the same," he said. "Never mind that, the Vichy practically have us trapped here anyway."

24

Seek out the good in all the bad.

Palo Alto, CA

"What happened to your dad?" I asked Grandma when she first told me her story when I was a boy. She opened a can of cat food for Washo her cat and he rubbed against her leg. In the background Grandpa chuckled at the TV.

"I never found out," Grandma said. "But your parents named you for him. Do you know where 'Aaron' comes from?"

"No."

"Aaron was the older brother of Moses. His spokesman. It's an ancient Egyptian name."

"Were they Jewish?" I asked. At the time I didn't know what was Jewish or what was Christian. It was all new to me. Grandma nodded and gazed over the black and white photos standing in their frames on her shelf.

"The Nazis were known for taking meticulous records," Grandma said. "Every detail down to the last hair. But in Poland they weren't as thorough. Little is known about what happened to the people in the rural areas and the farms."

Grandma pulled out the atlas again and ran her finger down the dividing line pointing to Ranizow, Poland.

"My Father had the great misfortune of being a few miles to the left on this map. In the area controlled by the Nazis."

"Was he killed?" I asked. She only nodded.

"You see this picture, Aaron?"

Grandma took a photo album off the shelf. Flipped it open and pulled out a tattered photo placing it in front of me. The black and white photo is grainy and shows a group of men sitting around in chairs and a woman in an apron smiling with a group of girls next to her. I would never have thought much of it. The men wore white bands on their arms.

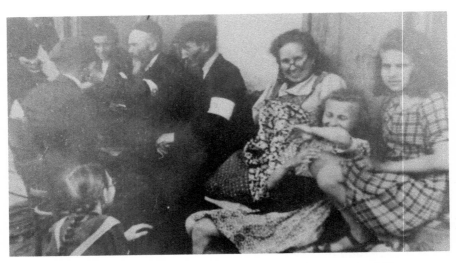

Photo of Aron, fifth from the right, taken by a Nazi soldier.

"Do you know what this is?" Grandma asked.

"What?"

"This is the last photo I have of my father," she said. "Your great-grandfather is the man in the center of the men with the beard and Yamaka. He's reaching for an apple and on his arm do you see that white armband?"

I focused on the picture and saw my great-grandfather's long, greying beard and the white sash on his arm.

"That's the Star of David armband. The Nazis made Jews wear

those."

"Why?"

"So they knew who was a Jew."

"He sent it to you?"

"His sister, Dora, received it in the mail. The letter was from a Nazi soldier."

"A Nazi sent it?" I was confused.

"Yes, the Nazis started going on patrols through the farmland after the invasion and one day the soldier encountered father out front of a village general store. The soldier took some pictures, like we might do in a zoo. A souvenir. Your great-grandfather was in deep discussion with family and friends, but he noticed the soldier snapping photos. 'Hello,' my father said in German. 'You can come over.' He offered him an apple.

"'How did you learn German so well?' the soldier asked. My father always said you learn a lot from the questions people ask. Perhaps he saw something in the soldier's question.

"'My sister, Dora lives in Chemitz,' Father said. It turned out the soldier was from Chemitz too.

"'I'll send a photo to your sister if you give me her address,' the soldier said.

"'Thank you, sir.' Father wrote it down. The soldier could have done many things with that address.

"However, weeks later Aunt Dora found a letter in her mailbox with the photo. The soldier kept his promise and told her of the pleasant encounter with father. I think of my last dinner with father and my last time with him."

Grandma picked the photo up and held it with her small fingers. She studied it and set it back down.

"The woman smiling in the photo is my aunt, and those girls are my cousins. They look as if they have no idea what is coming."

Grandma's green eyes had a mist encasing them and she wiped the creases at the corners of her lips.

"Maybe it wasn't the grandest act, but that German soldier did a decent thing sending this photo. It's the last picture or news I ever received about my father. He vanished from this world like so many others.

"There are good and bad from every country and culture. I've met my fair share of Jewish shysters. So even now I have a soft spot for this German. He gave me one last glimpse of my father."

The smell of grandma's soup wafted around the small house pulling her back into the moment and grandpa's chuckle broke the tension. She got up to stir the pot, tasting it, and dropped in a pinch of spice.

25

Don't give them a reason.

Marseille, France

The road was quiet in the dampness of early morning. Annie crossed a field to bypass police on the outskirts of Luchon. At the main road she checked for car lights that headed towards Toulouse. It was a long journey to Marseille hitchhiking. Carrying only a small bag of food mother gave her and the documents for the U.S. visa, she flagged down passing cars as the moon broke over the mountains and the night shadows emerged.

The Vichy French now arrested foreign Jews based on age, and Annie was over the age limit of 16. She was almost 20. The urgency to leave France was growing amongst Jewish refugees as the Vichy passed more decrees targeting them.

It didn't take long before a car pulled over. An older man looked at Annie inspecting her. "Where are you going?" the man mumbled in a French accent that was hard to understand.

"Marseille," Annie said.

"I can take you as far as Carcassonne," is what Annie gathered from the man's mumbles.

As his car crawled into Carcassonne and down side streets, a medieval castle rose into her view atop a mountain. Annie had heard about the castle, but to see it was like something out of a fairy tale father read her when she was young. It was one of the largest walled cities in Western Europe. The old man pulled over and waited for her to step out without saying a word.

Annie gazed at the castle, its turrets and stonewalls reaching high into the sky and stretching into the distance. Then she put her head down and walked towards Marseille. A farmer with crates of produce picked her up and took Annie the rest of the way.

The French seaport was bursting with businessmen, sailors and travelers from around the world. As the truck drove through mountains into the outskirts of Marseille, Annie saw the sea and miles of docks jammed with all sorts of ocean vessels; steam ships, skiffs, trawlers, and barges clogged the waterways. On land in the middle of unending rows of pastel buildings was a large hill with a white church sitting as a reminder to the city's rowdy sailors to behave.

Refugees from across Europe swamped the port city after the Nazi invasions, but instead of finding escape, they were relegated to the peripheries and tormented by the ships leaving the harbor towards freedom. It was like a black hood was pulled over the city as desperate refugees—now seeing the enormity and bleakness of their situation—flooded the city's nooks and crannies for any available space. Ocean liners sat in the harbors bound for New York, Canada, Argentina, but the odds for the thousands of people stuck in Marseille's arcades and back alleys were not good; it was near impossible to be granted passage on one.

But Annie had the documents from the Hassenfelds under her arm. She had made the proper copies the embassy required, and now she just needed to get inside the embassy to present their application. Hopefully mother's cousin had retrieved the ticket to get her in. Mother assured her he would show up. She walked down a narrow boulevard of row houses with shutters closed and plaster chipping from the sea air. There were some vagrants poking around in the shadows, drunks with nowhere to go. Annie skirted them and spotted a bus depot ahead.

A *gendarme* patrolled outside giving Annie both comfort and unease. She hid her eyes and moved quickly to the bus doors after he passed. Dockworkers stared as she climbed up the steps, but they returned their half-cocked gaze to the backs of their eyelids as the bumps in the road gently rocked them back to sleep. The bus billowed diesel smoke through the neighborhood side streets and Annie wondered what New York was like. Where was she supposed to meet her cousin? At the bench in the promenade outside the embassy? She studied his letter again not wanting to leave anything to chance.

The chaos outside the U.S. Embassy made the Portuguese consulate appear minor. It seemed to Annie that the world showed up here today. Thick lines of people stretched from two massive arched doors wrapping in both directions along the sidewalk, making it impassable. The embassy wouldn't be open for hours, but as morning light crept down the large building, the hoards of refugees swelled. A pit formed in Annie's stomach. The shear scope of the masses was intimidating, and they all wanted the same thing: To get inside, to get a visa, to survive. They would do anything for it. There was only one thing that kept Annie from turning around and retreating to Luchon. It wasn't the documents from the Hassenfelds or getting the U.S. visa. It was the fear of failing mother.

Where was the bench outside the embassy? Annie looked through the people, and pushed through the men standing in line. All she saw were more people, but no bench. She didn't know what her cousin looked like, but kept searching. There was a row of trees that lined the street and she walked all the way down the block. Nothing.

Just to the right of the embassy she saw a bench, but it was empty.

"What time is it, *monsieur?*" Annie asked a man standing in line.

"10 to 8," he said. Ten minutes! She had ten minutes to get the ticket. She sat at the bench and waited with the documents resting on her lap. Crowds of men came from every direction descending on the embassy and the bench was soon swallowed into the mass of people in a matter of minutes. Annie looked at each new face scanning for any hope of recognition.

"Annie," a man said from behind. She jumped up.

"Yes!"

"Sorry I'm late. The crowds made it hard to get here." He shoved the ticket in her hand.

"Thank you."

"Go! Find your spot."

Annie pushed through the immense throngs not knowing which direction to go, but she saw the embassy door amid the bodies and aimed for it. Ahead was a policeman and she had no choice but to ask him. The embassy was opening and her spot in line was in jeopardy.

"Excuse me, officer," she said to the tall *gendarme*. She stuck out the numbered ticket. "Am I in the right line with this ticket?"

"No, no," he said and Annie's heart skipped a beat. He looked closely at it. "You are at the front. Let her through!" he yelled and pointed to where she needed to go, which was near the arched doors. People moved out of her way as the policeman directed.

When the consulate doors opened seconds later Annie was one of the first to enter the sterile lobby smelling of cleaners used in government buildings and schools.

She sat with men on the benches. It was silent and a stark difference from the scene outside. She looked at her ticket, "209." A framed picture of Franklin D. Roosevelt, president of the United States hung on the wall and the ticking clock broke the silence. Annie wondered if the alarm clock that mother made her carry even worked? Would mother make her carry it to the United States?

"Number 209," a secretary called out in English. There was silence. "Is there a number 209?" the voice repeated now in French. The secretary was quick and ready to move to the next number.

"I'm here," Annie choked out in French. She didn't speak English. "I have 209."

"Step up miss," the woman said in French. "Quick, please. Do you have your documentation and paperwork filled out?" Annie brushed the wrinkles from her dress and pushed her hair behind her ears. She wore a white bow in her hair and a navy blue dress with a collar.

"I do, right here, thank you," said Annie pulling the papers out for the woman to see. The woman checked to make sure that there were the proper number of copies of the visa application (six copies), birth certificates (a quota system was put in place based on birthplace), the "Affidavit of Support and Sponsorship" (six copies) including the sponsor's tax returns and bank statements.

"Please show her in," she said to a tall, heavy-set man wearing a dark suit. "Number 210. You're next."

"Right this way, Madam," the man said. Annie walked through the dark, wood paneled hallway. Other refugees sat at desks with interviewers asking questions. Annie felt the dread of judgment.

"This gentleman will review your case." Annie thought she heard the man say the immigration officer was named, Wright. She stepped around the tall man.

Sitting at a small desk among rows of other immigration officials was Mr. Wright. He wore a simple, starched white shirt and dark blue tie. His face was shaved close with minor nicks on his chin and his hair combed with care, a part on the side. Annie noticed all of this and the aftershave he wore. It was this man who held her family's fate.

"Good morning, *monsieur*," she smiled and sat down at his desk.

He forced a smile and sat watching Annie pull out her documents saying nothing, his hands folded under a metal lamp. She fumbled the documents dropping papers on the floor. Mr. Wright observed her as she scrambled to pick them up. His expression remained unchanged; eyebrows flat and his eyes indifferent.

"I have all the required documents," Annie said stuttering over her words and putting the crinkled papers back together. He took the first paper from her.

"Do you speak English?" he asked in French.

"No, but I want to learn," Annie said. He scanned over the paper Annie gave him.

"To be clear, the visa applications are for a Blima Schmidt, a Sara Schmidt, a Hannah Schmidt and a Zlata Schmidt?" he said. Annie watched his expressions trying to decipher his thoughts.

"Yes," Annie said.

"Passports and birth certificates, please." He put out his hand in a rote motion. Annie handed them over.

"What's your country of origin?"

"We're from Antwerp, Belgium," Annie said, "but I was born in Germany as was my sister, Zlata."

Wright said nothing reviewing the paperwork.

"Where was Blima Schmidt born?" It said it right there on the application.

"She was born in Bojanow, Poland."

"What relationship is she to you?"

"She is my mother."

"What language does she speak?"

"Polish, German, Yiddish, and Hebrew."

"Where is your father? He is not on your application."

"We don't know," Annie said. "He was in Poland during the Nazi invasion."

Wright didn't lift his eyes from the paper as he asked the questions in a routine sequence that was well practiced. Annie looked hard at him and listened to his questions, but didn't have a grasp on his thoughts. She went over all the paperwork in her mind as he looked at them trying to search out any possible hiccups he might see on the documents.

The questions from Wright went to the extended family, and acquaintances. Annie knew the answer to every single question and the background.

"Why do you want to enter the United States?" Wright said having worked his way through most of the documents. Annie was polite and quiet through his examination, and she thought about her answers and had even rehearsed.

"We want to join our family in Rhode Island," she said. "We seek political asylum and safety from the Germans and the Vichy French."

"I see you have a sponsorship letter from Henry and Herman Hassenfeld, in Providence, Rhode Island. They need to show sufficient funds to support your family."

"I have their bank statement right here." Annie handed the financial paperwork to Wright. "As you can see they have a very large sum of money."

He took the document and skimmed it over noting the bank sum. His expression hadn't changed from the moment she sat down until he came to the bottom of the page. His brows furled and he stared for a moment. Annie sensed there was something wrong in the way his eyes squinted over the paper. She assumed he was surprised at such a large sum, but that wasn't something to worry about. She knew that the tax returns and bank statements corresponded.

"Just one moment, please," Wright said and stood up taking the pages with him to an office with a name on the door, "Vice-Consul."

Annie listened to other refugees plead their cases to immigration officials around her for several minutes, and then Wright emerged from the office. He sat down in front of Annie with the bank statement placing it in front of her.

"Here's the problem, Miss Schmidt," he said in an even tone pointing to the bottom of the page. "This bank statement requires two signatures, and only one of the authorized signers has signed it. You need the other Hassenfeld signature."

"But the bank statement shows more than sufficient funds," she said as Wright's eyes paused on her. "You can see the Hassenfelds' willingness to support us in their letter and more than enough money. It's a small omission that means little to the merit of their account. Please, it took more than a month to get these documents."

"The bank statement is missing a signature," Wright said in the same even tone. "We cannot accept it, which makes your application incomplete." He stamped the paperwork with a red English word, but Annie understood full well what it meant. He rejected the visa application. Annie stared the man in the face.

"You understand that you have condemned my family to death? Over a technicality!" Tears streamed down her face and her lip quivered. "Do you understand that? Do you care that my family very well could die because you denied it over a missing signature? The other signature is there!" The big man from the refugee camp had warned her and she knew better. But what bothered her was that if it weren't for that missing signature, Wright would've found something else. His job wasn't to grant visas, it was to reject them.

"I will have somebody show you out," Wright said. The tall, heavyset man was standing next to Annie and as if on cue, he escorted her through the desks of other Jewish refugees into the lobby and outside. It was all a haze from there as she stepped on the sidewalk amidst the optimistic hordes waiting to get inside. But there was little hope of a U.S. visa for them either. The requests that made it inside were sent through the motions, stamped, and the refugees shown back out the door.

It was as if a punch landed in her gut and her head swiveled around for its bearings and to suck in air. "I can disappear," she said out loud to herself. It was as if her words woke her from the stupor and she pushed by the people.

Annie sat on a wood piling hugging her body for warmth. It was still early in the morning. What was she going to tell mother?

The large waterfront promenade wrapping around the inlet was packed with yachts and large avenues funneled down into this international access point. Annie watched people go in and out of buildings and to boats.

She tried to see a way out for her family, and her head pounded into the outer layers of her skull. Writing the Hassenfelds for the signature? It would take months. The U.S. immigration officials would find another reason to deny the application. Annie wiped the tears from her eyes and turned to watch a large sailboat navigate the obstacles of the docks, floating past a large stone citadel protecting the harbor and into safer waters of the Mediterranean. It looked so easy.

Part of her didn't want to return to Luchon and mother who waited. Annie stood up and stepped into the crowds of people commuting to work on La Canebiere Avenue. She found a transit station where there was a bus to Toulouse. There was just enough money for her to buy a ticket.

26

There are always glimmers of hope.

Luchon, France

Letty knew as soon as Annie opened the door and closed it without a peep trying to evade attention.

"How could you fail?" mother asked, not yet fuming mad because her shock hadn't subsided yet. "This was important. You realize that? This was our chance." She still held out hope that this was just a set back.

"There was a missing signature on the Hassenfelds' bank statement," Annie said. "They rejected our application because of that. There was nothing I could do. Nothing any of us could do."

"Write them! Get the signature!" Mother's voice rose in exasperation still clinging to her hope of a new life. She was perplexed that Annie didn't just remedy the situation. It seemed a valid option. Letty remained quiet trying to understand the situation.

Suzy walked through the door and stared at mother's face, red and bulging. Then she saw Annie's face, puffy and wet with tears.

"You can get the signature!" mothers said with a sharp tongue.

"It's not that simple," Annie said.

"It's not? Why wouldn't it be? We spent a good chunk of the money we have on your travel expenses." She pointed at the alarm clock sitting on a shelf irritated at Annie's unwillingness to make a simple fix like getting another signature. "We have sponsors in America waiting to support us!"

"Mother, there were thousands of refugees at the consulate trying to get a visa. All probably with sponsors. Mobs of desperate Jews just like us. These officials are looking for any reason to deny our application. If not the signature, then the fact that Letty and I were born in Germany." Nothing Annie said could help bring back the hope that was being extinguished with each word she uttered.

"Excuses!" Suzy said. "That's all you have! You are just going to throw away our one chance to get to America?"

"Suzy!" Letty said. "You do nothing, and then blame Annie for trying to help? You share nothing, yet expect us to share everything!" Their screams bounced off the walls of the little room and into the hotel's halls.

"You're one to talk," she said. "You run around with boys all day like you're on vacation. At least I'm working with a Belgian soldier who is making plans and joining the French resistance. What are you doing?"

Letty's face turned red. Mother's stare brought Letty's shame to the surface like the fat from a curdling stew. Mother's scarf that covered her head fell to her shoulders. Her hair was short, but it amplified the rage in her steel grey eyes. The *scheitel* she wore since Letty was a child was too damaged and dirty, and it lay in a heap under her cot.

"Enough!" mother yelled. "Annie, you will write the Hassenfelds to get that signature. Do it now! I will watch you write it!"

Annie sat down at the end of a cot facing the white wall and scribbled on paper. Her back shook as she cried to herself. Mother stood over her unable to read the French words Annie wrote. When she finished mother turned and went to her cot.

Letty remembered a letter had come for Annie earlier and grabbed it. "Annie," she said sitting next to her. "This came for you."

Annie looked at the writing on it and smiled. Opening the envelope she pulled out the letter and read it.

"Who's it from?" Letty asked.

"It's from Toby," she said in a whisper. "She's in Montauban." She looked at Letty. "It worked. I wrote letters to all the places Toby and her family could have gone. Seven letters. One of them found her."

27

Not everyone plays by the same rules.

They were woken at daybreak by a beating drum. Their eyes were groggy as they put their heads out the window to see what the commotion was about. The town "crier," a lame man with a red drum marched on a peg leg limping and pounding rhythmically with a stick. His runt dog, which resembled him with short legs and barreled torso, toddled alongside with a faint limp too.

"Listen here! Listen here!" he cried. "A public announcement at 9:00 am! All refugees must gather at the public square!"

"What's he saying?" mother said.

"We need to go to the town center," Letty said.

"Listen here! Listen here!" he cried in French, his drumbeat waking people from their slumbers in the village.

"Why?" mother said.

"He didn't say."

Suzy, Annie, mother and Letty waited for the announcement at the town center. More people flowed in from the hotels and other refugee lodging until it was packed. Chatter was rampant with speculation about the announcement. People spoke Flemish, Yiddish, French, Polish, German and Letty listened to all the flying rumors. She looked around for Theo and spotted him with his family. His floppy hair hid his eyes and he didn't see her. Near him was his friend, Daniel, who waved to Letty. She also looked for the police amongst the crowd.

The town "crier" hobbled up the stairs out front of a large building so that he saw the faces that gathered. He unfolded his paper looking it over and his dog took its place next to him.

"By order of the mayor all refugees are to gather at the train station tomorrow, no later than 10:00 in the morning with all their belongings," he said. His vocal cords strained to reach the faces in the back of the square. A wave of murmurs rose up across the crowd as they processed the extradition. Letty looked at Theo who seemed unmoved by the announcement.

"What did he say?" mother said.

"We have to leave Luchon tomorrow," Annie said.

"Where to?" she said. "Why?"

"They didn't say," Letty said. "Just to have our bags packed." Panicked faces conversed throughout the square. What did it mean? Where were they going?

Suzy left in an instant looking for the Belgian soldier and pushed through the people around her, "Excuse me, *monsieur*." Her soft smile softened her hard shoves and the people she brushed by didn't seem to mind moving out of her way.

Could they stay? Was that possible? These were questions Annie, mother or Letty didn't ask. They walked back to the hotel assuming they had to pack their things and leave. Mother gave Annie the alarm clock to put in her bag. Only a few of Suzy's things remained laid out. The door opened and Suzy stepped in trying hard to conceal a smile.

"Mother," Suzy said. "Because of Rudy's service in the Belgian army they're allowing him to stay here, in Luchon. He asked if I could stay? I told him, 'yes.'"

"What do you mean, Suzy?" mother said.

"I'm not going with you in the morning. Don't worry, I'll keep in touch and meet up with you as soon as possible."

"Are you sure you will be okay? Will it be safe?"

"Yes, mother," Suzy said. "He has assurances it's okay. They like that he's a soldier."

108

"You are staying?" mother said it again, trying to believe the words.

Letty went looking for Theo with the feeling of a knife in her gut. She knew where to find him. He no longer sat at the entrance of the Saccron bouncing his ball. Now he chose a spot closer to the cluster of trees that was hidden from foot traffic and cars.

"The mayor got rid of us after all," Letty said when she saw him. "I wonder where they are sending us?" Theo had his book, but wasn't reading. He sat staring at the road.

"My family isn't leaving."

"How?"

"My father worked it out."

Letty said nothing, but her shoulders slumped and her stomach twisted; both Suzy and Theo were staying.

They hugged and she buried her face into his chest to wipe the tears.

"I'll write you," Letty said. "My mother is waiting."

28

Find the hole in the fence.

Toulouse, France

A large number of refugees stood at the train station's platform with their suitcases as ordered. There were several policemen in high boots and cylinder hats congregating in the middle of the platform. Letty lost her breath when she saw the same policeman that questioned Theo and her at the spa, now positioned in the corner of the station in a dark brown suit. He motioned to the other police to fan out as he held a little notebook and jotted in it with a pencil.

A whistle blew in the distance and puffs of smoke spewed on the horizon as the train chugged into sight. Suzy didn't come to the station to see them off fearing the police. Mother's nerves were fragile and she shook as the locomotive rumbled up to the terminal. She had a scarf tied around her hair now that her wig was in the garbage.

Railway workers slid doors open to the cattle cars hitched to the train engine and attached long wood planks with wood slats crossing them. Policemen encircled the refugees and pushed them up the planks into the cattle cars. Some panicked and asked the *gendarmes* why they were being moved.

"Don't worry," a policeman said. "We have to move you because there's not enough food to sustain you here. You are going to a nice place with sheets and good food."

There were no seats or windows in the cattle car except for two open shutters at the top letting in air. The Schmidts stood packed in with the other refugees not knowing where they were going. The door slid closed behind and locked. The car was dark except for the light rays that shot through the cracks between the wood slats and air holes.

"Where are we going?" mother said.

They rocked forward as the train sighed leaving the station. Letty sat on her suitcase. Others asked in Flemish if the police said where they were going. She looked at Annie in the darkness, but Annie stood quiet, trapped in her mind, blaming herself for the visa rejection.

"I don't know," Letty said to mother. "They didn't say."

The train rattled on for an hour and slowed to a stop. There was yelling outside and the door slid open and light flooded into the car blinding them. When Letty's eyes adjusted she saw horse drawn wagons waiting. Railway workers and police shouted to move down the ramp and they pulled and pushed them.

"Where are we?" Letty asked a policeman.

"You'll find out," he said. "Let me help you into the cart." He grabbed her arm lifting her up. "All Jews into the wagons!"

A driver slapped the reins down and the horses jerked pulling them towards an unknown destination. In a desolate clearing in the distance was a cropping of long barracks. The wagons swayed nearer and Letty saw a tall chain linked fence with barbed wire surrounding the buildings and little moving specks, people barely visible in a muddy field. The passengers' heads were all stretching to see this place. The convoy of wagons turned down a long road that stretched through the fence line and to the center of the long white barracks. In the center of the dirt and mud quad were three policemen waiting at a table. The wagons came to a stop.

"Line up with your papers!" a *gendarme* said. "Line up!"

They climbed down the wagons and police separated them between men and women. It took hours it seemed with only two policemen taking their information. Mother was anxious and kept looking down the line at the man taking the passports.

"This place is terrible," mother said to anyone around her that listened. "Where are we?"

The internment camp was just south of Toulouse and was called Récébédou, which was newly established by the Vichy Government for Jewish and Spanish refugees, or so the rumors flying up and down the line said. When the mayor of Luchon had learned that the camp was now available for Jews he had made arrangements for his Jewish refugees to be transported there. He wasn't able to send them to Spain, but he was able to intern them here.

The policeman took their papers writing names in a ledger under "Juif," French for Jew, and assigned barracks for men and women. The place smelled stale with sickness and dirty flesh. Most of the people in the barrack were from the Spanish civil war. They were missing arms and legs, wearing bandages, and they laid suffering in beds of straw with horse blankets to keep them warm. Some of the Spaniards walked to the shared toilets on crutches, but none went outside which was why the muddy expanse was empty of people. Letty's family found their place in the straw and mother paced, unwilling to sit in the dirty mess.

"There are insects and fleas everywhere," she said. "I will not sleep here."

"There is nowhere else," Letty said. She sat down in the straw to show her it was okay. "At least it's not a bare floor." Mother shook her head like an obstinate child, folded her arms and kept pacing. She had had enough of sleeping in hay. There was a damp coolness in the air and the rains made everything in the barrack a pigsty.

Women dressed in white aprons, nurses for the injured, served stew out of large pots in an outdoor chow line. Food was scarce, but mother still refused to eat the plate that was handed to her.

"You need to eat," Letty said. Mother stared at the food contorting her face in revulsion.

"No, no, it's not Kosher," she said. "I cannot eat it." Letty also put her plate down as did Annie, but mother lifted them and pushed them in their hands.

"You eat," she said. "I want you to have your strength. It's okay." Annie and Letty ate on a bench as mother paced not wanting be near the food and disgusted by the grime of the camp.

"Mother won't last here," Letty said as she ate the chunks of animal fat in the stew. Pork? She didn't know what it was, but she was so hungry that it tasted good.

"May I sit?" a young man said speaking French to Annie. She nodded, yes, and he sat. "Where are you from?"

"Antwerp," she said.

"So am I," he said. "The food is not so good, but at least they provide it."

"No," she said. "It's not kosher. My mother refuses to eat."

"I see," he said looking at mother wandering up and down amongst the other refugees who were eating.

The man leaned over to Annie in between bites and spoke in Flemish. "There's a way out," he said in a whisper. His neck was long like his arms and legs. "There's a gap in the fence they haven't fixed yet."

"Where?" Letty said. She looked at the young man's face and dark mop of hair to gauge the seriousness of his words. His nose was big, but elegant and he had a little patchy facial stubble, unable to grow a full beard. His jacket was too small for him as his arms stuck out showing his wrists.

"The northwest corner behind the infirmary," he said scooping up the last bite of stew with his spoon and wiping the bowl with his fingers. "I hear they're going to fix the fence next week. They are moving the materials in. They haven't been too worried because there have only been a bunch of maimed Spaniards living here so far." Letty still tried to discern if he was putting them on, trying to impress Annie or if it was the truth.

"Why haven't you left already?" Letty asked.

"Where am I to go?" he said. "There's food here and a place to sleep.

But I may."

"The food's not kosher," Annie said.

"Food is food in times like this. Look, you're eating it." He examined his plate for anything he may have missed. "I'll leave when I decide which direction I'm going. But now, there's no telling where to go—"

"How do we get to Toulouse?" Letty said.

"There's a major road with a streetcar," he said. Annie pushed mother's plate of food over to the man. He ate the food inhaling it in a matter of seconds not hiding his loud chewing. He stared at them as he swallowed. There were bits of stew on his lip and chin. He leaned in. "Have you heard about Switzerland?"

"No," Letty said.

"They say they'll offer asylum."

"What's that?"

"You don't have to worry they'll give you to the Nazis."

"Are the French doing that?—"

"Asylum?" he said. "No. You haven't heard anything about Switzerland?"

Letty shook her head.

"The French are turning people over to the Nazis?" she asked.

"Oh, it's just rumors," he said. "What about Spain?"

"People tried to cross at the border and they turned them back."

"I heard about that. You can't cross the border without the proper papers. But you can hike across where no one is looking." The man was now wiping the remnants off of Annie's plate.

"That's not easy for families to do," Annie said.

He got up when he finished cleaning off all their food. Letty watched him walk across the muddy field to his barrack. Others returned to the shacks where they slept. It was cold and Letty pulled her sweater up around her neck.

"Should we look for the opening?" Annie said.

"Tonight," Letty said. "We need to get through that fence."

In an instant they decided to go despite no plan and nowhere to go.

As they slopped through the thick, gooey mud back to the barrack they told mother the plan to leave through the hole in the fence. It confused her and she looked at them like they were crazy.

"That's too dangerous," she said. "What if they catch us?"

Their only alternative was stay at the camp. By the time they walked into the flea infested sleeping area next to the injured Spaniards smelling of sickness and pungent body odor, mother was willing to entertain the idea.

"We will look at it only," she said. "To see if it's safe."

As the moon started to rise and the sun lowered casting silhouettes on the horizon, mother, Annie and Letty walked towards the infirmary. No one was out; only the lights in the barracks flickered. They left their suitcases back in the hay. Letty peeked around the building scouting what was out there. There were no guards and her feet slid in the mud trying to find solid footing. In the dark orange horizon of day's end they saw the gap in the fence. If you didn't know to look, you might not see there was an opening. Fresh rolls of wire and wood posts to make the repairs were scattered about. It was just as the young man said. The rain and cold weather probably prevented them from already patching the hole.

"Let's go," Letty said. Perhaps it was fear of missing their chance to flee the camp or the excitement of the moment. Letty pulled the loose fence back. Mother didn't argue and was the first to walk through, then Annie, and then Letty. It was as easy as that and they kept walking all the way to the main road in silence. It was hard to miss the lights of the streetcar station along the highway.

"We don't have our bags," mother said. "We need our things. Letty, you had us leave without our things! What are we going to do now? Where are we going to go?"

"I'll go back and get them," Letty said, unsure what else to do. She thought about all her options, but there was only one. "Mother, you and Annie wait here at the station. I'll get the bags."

"No, no!" mother said. "Don't be stupid. There is someone in

Toulouse I know from Antwerp. We will find them." Mother learned from the women at the Saccron Hotel that Mrs. Goldberg from their street in Antwerp had taken a small room with her sons in Toulouse. They climbed on the empty streetcar riding it into the city center. Mother was in quiet lament over her stranded suitcase.

The apartment building sat on a main square near the station. They climbed the staircase and mother knocked on the door. It opened a crack revealing an eyeball, the person behind careful to see who was there. Then it opened wide and Mrs. Goldberg stood with her arms out.

"Come in, come in," she said with a huge smile. "I almost didn't recognize you, Blima." Mother's scarf on her head was far different than the big wig she once wore.

The small room had two beds, but there was a kitchen and the walls were decorated with family pictures from Antwerp. Her two sons sat there staring at the girls.

"Where are your things?" Mrs. Goldberg asked.

"We came from a camp and left them," mother said. "Our suitcases were too heavy." Before they even sat down Mrs. Goldberg pointed to her son, a well-built young man.

"Can he help you pick them up?"

"Yes, he can," mother said. "Thank you. Letty, show him where they are." Letty hadn't even entered the apartment and she was already leaving on a streetcar back to the camp with Mrs. Goldberg's son.

"How long have you been in Toulouse?" Letty asked the boy, who was probably fourteen.

"Not long," he said.

"But you have an apartment?" Letty said.

"The Jewish community provided it. They give us money for food too."

"This is the stop," Letty said.

A half moon fighting through the overcast lit their way towards the camp on the damp night. Letty was lost when she came to the fence.

She didn't know which direction to go.

"There's a gap in the fence," she said. "I just don't know where it is."

She backtracked toward the front gate where a lone guard sat. He saw them before she had a chance to turn around.

"*Qui va là?*" the guard said. "Who goes there?"

"My family is in this camp," she said. "Please let me in."

He opened the gate letting them pass without any questions. The smell of the barrack wafted into her nostrils first, then her eyes adjusted. She found the bags sitting in the hay where they left them. Mrs. Goldberg's son covered his nose with his shirt.

Faces in the damp straw, illuminated by light coming inside from a flickering lamppost, spied them. Letty saw the whites of their eyes staring at her in the dark, blinking, but silent. She understood why the wounded were lying down, but wondered why the others chose not to go through the hole. The opening wasn't going to last forever.

They picked up the heavy suitcases and stayed close to the walls of the barracks. She led the way to the gap in the fence on the other side of the camp. It was pitch black now with the moon covered by thick clouds, except for the glow of a few lamps. There was no one but this boy and her walking in the night. She pulled the chain-link back for the boy. He carried two cases up the road to the station and she one.

29

Your demons are close, even if you pretend they aren't.

Washington, DC

"I'm sure it's good, but I can't watch it," grandma said. I had just seen the movie, *Schindler's List* and recommended it to her. She refused to watch or read anything about the Holocaust. It was a subject she preferred to put out of her mind. I knew my digging into her story conjured terrible feelings and memories, as did the topic of my mom's death. I didn't know how my grandma processed the loss. We didn't talk about it, and I knew she didn't believe in God. I had my own battles with the emotions surrounding the loss of my mom, and those hidden feelings had a funny way of revealing themselves.

When I went through the turmoil surrounding my mom's death I was too young to understand or to put my finger on what it was I was going through. All I saw was the chaos and aftermath of a life I had once known end before my eyes. I preferred to forget, pretend it didn't happen and stuff it away. It was my roommate's suicide that brought the painful reminder of that feeling.

My roommate, Puck, had an enormous personality that was only matched by his immense frame. He was so big, a sturdy six-foot-four, that when the coroners tried to carry his body down our steep and narrow hundred-year-old house they resorted to dragging his body through the tight opening of the stairs. His crown full of bushy black hair rustling inside the body bag thumped each step. Thump, thump, thump until they loaded him onto the gurney in our living room.

That image and thud noise resounded in my head every time I walked up those creaking stairs, but it was the empty space his sudden and tragic departure caused that reminded me of my childhood. His presence vanished, from his dark brooding to his booming laugh to the more tangible like his portion of the rent and bills. I thought about Puck each night when the panic was most intense, and the inner beast I feared to know tore at my chest.

His girlfriend, who found his body, still walked by the house, not coming to say hello, but staying across the street like a creeping ghost from the past. She didn't wave, only glanced at our red brick row house for a second and continued on with her life, never making eye contact, Puck still living in her memory. I wondered if my mom's friends ever wondered about me, that seven year-old boy they once took out to birthday dinner.

As I contemplated why Puck did it, knowing I was capable of the same, I couldn't shake the thought of my mom's own anguish understanding she was going to die, and the pain she must've felt knowing she was never going to see her little boy grow up. It gutted me thinking back to all those tubes that hung from her arms, and wondering how hard she fought to live, if she could have made it. I wanted to tell her, sorry, and that I didn't know what possessed that kid to spit. I wanted to tell her how much I loved her. I wanted to say goodbye.

For the first time I knew what drew me to grandma's story like a flailing moth. I wanted to be close to my mom. I wanted to impress her, to make her proud, and in a strange way I had made grandma her surrogate.

30

Find a footing in the void.

Lourdes, France

In the center of town was a Catholic Basilica with three Gothic towers pointing to the sky. Rumors had it Lourdes was a safe haven for Jews. The mayor received information about *razzias*, Vichy raids on Jews and tipped off the refugees. It was the monasteries and churches where they were to go if the police came for them. But the main reason they travelled to Lourdes was Suzy. She had traveled there with the Belgian soldier.

A large cross hung on the wall of their motel room, which mother covered with a scarf as soon as she entered. The Schmidts were running out of money and relied on aide from a Jewish relief organization, which provided just enough money to pay for the room and some bread and cheese for a couple weeks. Blima set up candles below the draped cross, insisting on lighting them for Shabbat while Letty kept a nervous look out the window through the curtains.

Out on the street a man loaded boxes into the canvas-covered flatbed of a truck. When Letty pulled the shades back, he looked up and saw her watching from the window and she flipped her hair back pretending she wasn't spying the people on the street.

"Hey *fille*!" he yelled up at her. "I'm much better up close! Spare a moment?" He puckered his wet lips at Letty. She threw the shades

120

down and ran to the door, leaving mother by herself.

"Where you going?" mother said, yelling after her.

"Out of this room," Letty said, shutting the door.

Annie was in the lobby playing bridge with a couple named Nussbaum. Felix Nussbaum was a painter from Germany. He was a prodigy forced to flee the country when Hitler took power. His place as a rising artist was meaningless to the Nazis who saw him only as a Jew. His high forehead and sharp nose projected the intensity not felt in his soft words. There was sadness in the dark hollows of his eyes. His wife, Felka, also an artist, was a chain-smoker and had a face that said she had seen and done everything. She moved like a dancer as she got up from the bridge game to light another cigarette. Letty never met such a woman in the confined Jewish company her mother kept. Blima, Letty and her sisters were short, sturdy, and blended in wearing dresses that melted into the background. Felka was the opposite of the Schmidt girls.

The Nussbaum's spoke in song, their intense words rhyming together as if they were depicting the painting of the frenzied world they saw.

"Darling," she said to Felix in German, "aren't these girls such innocent flowers? They remind me of the *belle ragazze* strolling the arcades of Rome coaxing young boys with their delicate smiles."

He grinned grabbing a book from the table and thumbing its pages looking for something. Annie looked at the hardbound spine not able to read the title. He found a piece of paper with a small sketch of a world-globe resting on a table and in the distance a man sitting with his head in his hands. There was nothing in the bare room but a cane and a hat. Letty looked at the picture feeling its emptiness.

"What language is that book?" Annie asked.

"English."

"You can read English?" she said, cringing at the memory of the American immigration official.

"I can," he said. "It's not an easy language to learn. It has a large and tricky vocabulary and the grammar is packed with subtlety." He set his sketch on the table and started reading the book out loud, "Shhh shhh shhh," is all Letty heard, like snakes hissing. She looked more closely at the picture tuning out the words. "It's an important language to know. Would you like to learn?" he said to Annie.

"Sure—"

"What's this picture?" Letty asked.

"It's the very first sketch of a painting I made, '*The refugee*,'" he said picking up the paper again and staring at it. "I keep it close as a reminder of the uprooted life I, we, live. Trapped in a world that neither claims nor wants us. Our families torn, fragmented and spread across the world in search of a place. We must live as they hunt us, unsure of what we did."

They sat quiet in the hotel lobby looking at the sketch of the globe and refugee, Felka's cigarette smoke wafting in their faces. The playing cards of the bridge game were scattered across the table.

"Sheesh," Felka said. "You are so morose. Felix, teach this young lady the garbles of English, or shuffle the cards. We mustn't stew in this abyss."

31

Self-interest has a cost.

"Dear Letty." She stopped to observe Theo's crisp handwriting. The paper smelled of citrus, like he peeled an orange before writing. "It's not the same without you here. Many refugees sent to the camp have returned to Luchon. But not you. I keep wondering if you will come back. I miss our hikes to the lake. I went up there last week, but it was cold and drizzled. Please let me know how you are doing. Theo."

Letty had sent Theo a letter when she arrived in Lourdes, and had waited for this letter. She responded the same day, but it was the last letter she received.

"Have you heard from Suzy?" mother said. Since they arrived in Lourdes, Suzy was also a mystery. Mother didn't know if something had happened to her. "Why hasn't she come? You told her we were here?"

"I left her a message at the address she wrote," Annie said, "but they said the Belgian soldier left."

"She has gone?" Mother paced the room gripping her fingers.

It was Christmas and the Gentiles flooded the streets in the evening with candles. Mother refused to see the spectacle. The streets sparkled like the Milky Way with endless flames running like a river all the way to the Basilica. It was for the miracle of Lourdes, when the Virgin Mary appeared to a peasant girl not once, but eighteen times. "It's a nice story," Letty said.

Annie and Letty followed the procession through the cobble stone paths, wax candles dripping over their hands, and down the large avenues turning into a sea of flickering lights. Letty stopped. She stared and then blinked her eyes thinking her eyes were playing a trick in all the candle lights. She grabbed Annie's arm and pointed, not believing what she was seeing.

"What are you doing?" Annie said.

Standing across the street watching the procession was Suzy. Letty scanned the area for the Belgian soldier, Rudy, but he was nowhere to be seen. Suzy was like a stranger in the crowd with her hair fixed up. Her bangs puffed high over her forehead and she wore make-up that was different. Her jacket and dress were brand new. If Letty hadn't grown up with her, she wouldn't have recognized her.

"What is it, Letty?" Annie said.

"Look. There's Suzy." She pulled Annie through the people and candles avoiding the burning hot wax. As they got near, Suzy stepped into the flowing street of lights with an older couple and disappeared. They watched their sister melt away into the night and had no idea what Suzy was up to until she appeared at their door a few days later. She must have sensed they knew.

"Suzy!" mother said throwing her hands out. "I've missed you so much. Are you okay?"

"Here's some chocolates for you," Suzy said, handing a fancy box to mother. "I've missed you too."

"How are you?" mother said. "Let me take a look at you. You are dressed so nice."

"Rudy joined the French resistance," Suzy said.

"So come back and stay with us," mother said.

"I have a place. A family from Paris, the Richfelds, adopted me as their daughter."

"What do you mean?" mother said.

"From this day forward I am no longer part of this family. The Richfelds will take care of me from now on. Don't worry, I will be well taken care of."

The blood drained from mother's face. She struggled to find words as her mouth flexed and was silent. Letty was confused too. "Suzy left our family?"

"It's okay," Suzy said. "They have lots of money and are able to buy plenty of food on the black market. I'll be okay. You will always be my mother, but now I have a stepmother too. And I won't be a burden on you."

Mother stared at the wall and her knees buckled and she sat back into a chair.

"If you leave Lourdes you can contact me here," Suzy said, placing a paper with her address on the table. "This is where I'll be living with my new family." With that she left without hugging mother goodbye. Perhaps it was more final that way. It was very bizarre, but the only thought Letty had was, "Good riddance. She was a terrible sister, so let the other family have her."

32

Don't waste time fighting perceptions that won't change.

"Farewell, Annie!" Felka shouted out the window of the car, blowing her a kiss, her wild eyes dancing like blue orbs. Annie put her hand up, then brought it down to her side. She didn't know about death camps at the time, or the severe consequences that faced Jews. Annie didn't know that Felix and Felka Nussbaum would be arrested and sent to Auschwitz where they would be killed. Those stories and rumors were not yet known, just that Jews were being hunted. Consequences of capture were only thought to be internment camps, like Récébédou or Drancy. However, it was those camps that would start shipping their prisoners to the Nazis.

When the Nussbaum's left, Annie moved on too. "I'm joining Toby in Montauban," she said to mother.

"You're leaving me?" mother said. She didn't raise her head from sewing the stitch in a dress. Annie gathered her things in a suitcase and closed the door of the room making only a rustle and squeak of the knob.

Mother was negative about almost everything, except a "young couple" she passed the days with. "They're so wonderful, and smart. I wish you could understand the world as they do," she said to Letty. "They see it so clearly." The only other person she spoke like that about, was Suzy. Even in her absence, Suzy was her "beautiful daughter."

"If Annie had not screwed things up at the U.S. embassy, Suzy wouldn't have been put in this situation," mother said. It was Annie who had stolen Blima's hope of a new life, not the American embassy.

Letty stayed in Lourdes waiting for the letter that would never come from Theo. A week later a letter did come, though from Annie urging them to join her in Montabaun. Local officials were sympathetic towards Jews she said. There was also the opportunity to make money through Toby's family connections.

Rumors about French police raids on Jews were increasing in cities around Vichy France. No one knew which cities were safe, and which weren't. Lourdes was as good as any, but in the end mother decided to travel to Montabaun, not because of Annie, but because the only person she trusted less than Annie, was Letty. This was how she made the decision. The fact they were broke and needed to make money was secondary.

"You're unreliable," she said. "You'll be the death of me. At least I can trust Annie not to kill me with stupidity. It's a rotten choice I have between you two."

33

Help comes from where you least expect it.

Days before the Jewish holiday of Purim Letty walked through the hotel lobby and onto the street looking for a ride to Montauban to meet up with Annie. They didn't have enough money for a train ticket and Blima refused to hitchhike. Letty circled town weaving through streets and over a bridge and then back.

The man that unloaded his truck every day in front of the hotel leered at Letty as he stacked crates. Letty remembered how he yelled at her and puckered his lips. He blocked cars with his cargo and they honked and yelled at him. He paid them no attention pulling his load off. Instead, he sang to himself and talked to people walking by, even if they ignored him. Letty tried to slip back into the hotel without him glimpsing her. By now she knew he was just a bloke with a wandering eye. Before she pushed through the hotel door she stopped and spun around walking back out on the street. She had an idea.

"Excuse me, *monsieur*," Letty said. "That's a nice truck. Do you ever drive to Montabaun?"

"Hello mademoiselle," he said. "That's a nice dress you wear. You fill it out in all the right spots." He grinned and set his crate down on a cart. Letty leaned against it. "For a pretty thing like you, I could." A car honked at him. "Quiet you!" His accent was rough. The car honked again and he ran over and smacked the grill. Then turned back to her. "Sorry, love. No respect."

"When are you leaving?" Letty said.

"You're very forward!" he said. "I like that. I'm leaving in two hours."

"Okay. I guess I can be ready then."

"A couple hours then," he said, winking. He had a large nose and sunken cheeks and the stocking cap on his head was pushed back exposing wispy brown hair. Letty crossed in front of the honking car and looked back at her new ride, giving him a wink.

"You have me by the heart!" He thumped his fist against his chest. Letty ran upstairs and put some lipstick on.

"I found us a ride," she said.

"Who?"

"A truck driver."

"Is it safe?"

"Yes, mother."

"It better be. Do you know the driver?"

"Yes."

"How?"

"He helps at the hotel."

With only their suitcases to pack they were down in the lobby in no time. They waited for an hour not saying a word until mother complained.

"Your ride is going to strand us," she said. "We are going to be left here."

The man pulled up in his truck and honked. He smirked when he saw Letty come out to the street.

"You showed up," he said. "My lucky day!"

"What's he saying?" mother said, coming up behind her and tugging at Letty's shoulder. The man looked at mother as if she was a leper.

"Is this woman bothering you?" he said putting his truck in neutral and about to get out.

"This is my mother," Letty said. "She's coming with us." His smile faded and he revved the engine like he was going to leave them right there. She jumped up and opened the door before he drove off leaning into the cab. "Don't worry, she doesn't speak French. It won't stop us from getting to know each other." She put her hand on his wrist. He looked down at her hand and smiled.

"What's he saying?" mother said. "Letty, tell me what he's saying!"

"We have a long drive ahead and need to get going."

Letty squeezed into the bench seat in the middle between mother and this Gentile. As he pushed the clutch into first they lurched forward, and then as he pulled the stick into second his hand slipped off and onto her leg. She glanced at mother who stared out the window, not happy with the truck or the Gentile, but unaware of anything else. Letty pushed his hand off playfully and smiled at him, not wanting to offend their host.

"Now who's forward," Letty said. "I don't even know your name." Mother swung her gaze from the passing street to her daughter. "He was just pointing at the traffic," Letty said to her in Yiddish.

"I'm Gustave," he said.

"His name is Gustave," Letty translated.

"I don't like the way he talks to you," mother said.

His truck grumbled and spewed smoke as they climbed into the mountains leaving Lourdes. With every shift of the clutch the man grazed the curve of Letty's thigh that was hidden under her dress.

"When will we have time for ourselves?" Gustave said. "I want to hold your hand."

"I'm dropping my mother off in Montaubaun. Maybe then?"

"What's he saying?" mother said. She grew suspicious. "Tell me what he's saying. I don't trust him."

"He's just telling me about his job," Letty said.

"When will that be?" he said.

"In a week."

"I can't wait that long," he said. "I want to feel your lips. And other places. Like your neck." He snickered.

"What's he saying now, Letty?"

"The drive gets long, but he likes the freedom," she said.

"It's nice to have you on this ride," Gustave said looking at Letty and not the road. The pavement curved into the jagged mountains and they were away from the world. "I know many secret spots to stop." Now Letty laughed, unable to keep it in.

"Letty, why are you laughing?" mother said.

"He joked that his truck acts like an old man in the mountains." She was enjoying the game.

"What language is your mother speaking?" he said. "I've never heard anything like it."

"It's Yiddish," she said. He looked over at mother and then Letty and turned his focus to the mountain pass.

"You speak a lot of languages?" he said.

"A few."

"Where are you from?"

"Belgium."

"I must make a stop," he said. "I have a message for my cousin." His truck turned off the main highway and bounced into a lower gear. Mother watched him, wary of his every move, and he watched her too as he shifted the clutch lower, his hand stayed on the stick rather than Letty's knee. They pulled into a tiny village.

"Where are we going?" mother said.

"I don't know. He's meeting his cousin."

The truck came to stop in front of a building. On it was a sign that read, "*Gendarmarie.*" Letty's heart raced as the man got out and went inside the police station. Mother was unaware of the dilemma unable to read French. Letty didn't dare tell her. Thoughts ran through her head, "Should I tell her we need to get out of the truck and run? I don't know where we are or what to do if we get out. Is he turning us in?"

"What is it?" mother said.

"Don't worry. He'll be back in a moment." Letty didn't know if it

131

was foolish to stay or flee. The door of the police station opened and he appeared with a woman in a uniform.

"Who is this?" mother said. "Police?"

"It's fine, mother," Letty said. But she wasn't sure if it was.

Gustave walked up with the woman and opened the passenger door. He needed mother to get out.

"He wants me to get out, Letty?" She looked at Letty with pleading eyes.

"This is my cousin," he said. "I need to give her a ride. She's pregnant and needs to sit in the cab."

"It's okay, mother. We need to go to the back of the truck."

"I'm an old woman."

"This woman is pregnant. You can stay if you like, but I need to go to the flatbed."

Letty climbed out giving the woman the cab, and mother followed like a child. It was a slow truck and what took a car a short time took them twice as long. They crawled up and over peaks and down through quaint French villages. She looked out the corner of the flap and they had stopped at an Inn. The flap was thrown open.

"We'll stay here for the night," Gustave said. It was dark, but Letty saw his grin. "I need to make a couple repairs to the truck. My cousin is the innkeeper and he'll take care of us."

They had their own room, but mother was beside herself, worried that Gustave was up to no good.

"You watch that truck all night," she scolded Letty. "He is going to leave us here."

"I'll watch," Letty said. "It'll be fine."

"Don't give me, 'It'll be fine,'" she said. "You got us into this mess. Don't leave that window." Letty sat there watching the truck hoping Gustave wasn't going to knock on their door. "If he sneaks off I'll wring your neck! I knew I shouldn't trust you. You're unreliable. An idiot! Why did I listen to you? We wouldn't be in this mess!" Mother was working herself into a manic mess. Nothing Letty said or did calmed her. It only made it worse.

"Mother, I'm nervous too. This isn't helping. Please relax."

"I don't care if you're nervous! You should be, you ignorant child! We're stranded because of you. We're left to fend for ourselves in who knows where? There's no one to help. I'm stuck with you! Stuck with you! You are going to be the death of us. I knew you'd be the death of me! I knew it!"

Letty tuned her out as best she could. Blima wasn't stopping and it was breaking Letty's nerves. Maybe she was going to get them killed. When you're told something enough you start to believe it.

"I keep putting up with your foolishness!" mother yelled. "It's going to be the end of us. Tonight is going to be the end of us. It's your entire fault! He's going to leave without us." Mother lay in the bed and watched Letty watch the truck. "Keep your eyes open, Letty! I'm not going to let you be the nail in my coffin. My own child's recklessness is going to kill me."

She just repeated herself over and over again and didn't stop berating Letty until the sun rose and the truck sat in the same spot unmoved. Gustave was checking the tires as they walked from the room with their suitcases. He lifted the bags into the back and they climbed into the cab. His pregnant cousin lived at the Inn.

"Sleep well?" he asked Letty. "I hoped you would've come say, 'hi.'"

"My mother wasn't feeling well, sorry," Letty said glancing at her mother whose arms clutched a small bag. She said nothing as they rolled down the hill toward Montaubaun.

Gustave pulled into a train station a little after mid-day where Annie had said to meet.

"When will I see you?" he asked.

"I don't know," she said. "Next week?"

"I drive by here next week. If you are here I will be happy. If not, you take care."

"What did he say?" mother said.

"He said for us to have a good trip."

133

He grabbed Letty's hand as she slid out of the truck. Part of her wanted to leave right then with him like Suzy had done, but she pulled her hand back and waved.

34

Some risks aren't worth the trouble.

Montaubaun, France

Toby Lerner was from a large family in Antwerp. Annie became friends with Toby at the Orthodox Jewish organization in Antwerp, and Letty knew her well from Behr's travel agency. Annie was drawn to the loose-knit nature of the Lerner family where people came and went with no control.

There were seven children in the Lerner family and Chayim, the fourteen year-old, stood up saying he had a joke to tell as Letty and Blima sat down at the dinner table.

"Go on, let's hear your joke," Mr. Lerner said.

"What's the difference between Jesus and a picture of Jesus?" he asked.

"What?" Mr. Lerner said.

"You only need one nail to hang a picture of Jesus!" he yelled.

The boys snickered and Letty looked over at Annie to gauge her reaction. She looked down trying not to smile. It was a crude joke for the dinner table, but Mr. Lerner thought it was great. He had a deep belly laugh drowning out everyone else. His head tilted back while he howled at the ceiling. Mr. Lerner was an Orthodox prig that reminded Letty of Abraham from the *Bible* with his bushy, unruly, white beard, and his sanctimonious behavior. He was old, reverent to his God, and if he spoke to women at all, it was to deride them.

"This food is terrible!" he said to his wife in front of his children and guests. "How could you serve this during Purim?" He picked his plate up with meaty fingers and dropped it on the table. "I'm embarrassed for you."

Dora Lerner was his second wife and her smile was kind and unflinching even with her husband's criticisms flying at her. She had a daughter named Leah from a previous marriage. Leah was Letty's age and sat next to her at dinner. She leaned over to Letty as her stepfather caught his breath between howls. "I have a job delivering eggs for a farmer," Leah said. "I can use a hand if you like." Letty didn't hesitate at the job offer.

Letty started wheeling eggs across town to houses and markets. She gathered the eggs in crates and then stacked them as high as possible in a wheel barrel while Leah steadied it. The more they amassed, the more money. It was on these trips Leah told Letty about her stepbrother.

"Josiah has these thick wads of cash," Leah said. Josiah Lerner was in his thirties and had connections with the black market making deliveries of all kinds throughout southern France. No one knew what he was delivering, only that it made him a lot of money.

"How does he make so much?" Letty said.

"I don't know. He's never offered a reason, and I don't ask."

The next day Letty went to meet Leah to haul eggs, but when she knocked it was Josiah who came out. He stared at Letty with his dark eyes. He had a chiseled chin and licked his lips a lot. There was a bulge under his leather jacket.

"Hello Letty," Josiah said, taking a quick survey of the street for any people. "Leah says you're looking to make some extra money. I have a job for you if you want?"

"I don't know. I already have a job with Leah."

"It'll be easy."

"What is it?"

"Deliver a package to Marseille. That's all."

"Why not do it yourself?" she said.

"Because I look too Jewish." Josiah had thick, dark hair that he combed to the side and a nose that hooked like a camel's, but she didn't think of him as looking Jewish. "You know how the police are arresting people for being Jewish. You don't look Jewish." He surveyed her dress, her dark brown hair, her full cheeks and thin lips.

"I don't look Jewish?" Letty asked.

"No, you could pass for a French girl. You want to do it or not? I can ask someone else." Letty blushed and smoothed out her dress.

"How much?"

"A thousand francs and I'll pay for your train fare." That was more money than Letty could make pushing eggs down the street and doing other odd jobs for months. It was an easy choice.

"Okay. What am I delivering?"

"It's a package. What's inside is none of our business. I don't even know what it is, but I'll give you 500 francs up front, and 500 when you return."

"When?"

"Now."

"I have things to do now. I have to make deliveries with Leah. I need to get some things."

"I'll tell her you won't make it. It has to be now. They're expecting it."

He reached into his jacket and pulled out train tickets and a package wrapped in butcher paper. It was the size of two novels, but a lot heavier.

"Keep it safe. Don't let anyone see it, and don't open it. See this seal. They'll know." He pointed at a stamp with a rooster pasted over the wrapping where the edges met. "Here's the address. It's near the train station."

"Is there a name?"

"No."

"Give it to anyone?"

"Deliver it to the restaurant! C'mon, if we leave now you can catch the train."

Josiah walked with her to the station and then watched Letty board. He gave her a cloth bag to put the package in. "If anyone asks you what it is, just say it's a present for your mother." She took her seat and tried to read his face on the platform, but he had no expression. There was something in the way he stared at the side of the train and licked his lips. He was lost in thought, or disinterested.

The train sighed and pulled away from the station and Josiah strolled away with his hands pushed into his jacket pockets. She had a six-hour train ride to Marseille. The bag rested on her lap and she wondered what was so heavy? She lifted it, knocked it with her knuckles and ran her fingers over the stamp that sealed the contents inside. The railcar was empty except for a few scattered passengers and she poked her head around the seats. After the conductor took her ticket Letty put her head against the window feeling the sway and rattle of the train. She shut her eyes forgetting about her job and fell fast asleep.

According to Josiah the restaurant was near the train station. Letty checked the timetable board and it showed the last return train to Montauban from Marseille was in an hour at 6:05 pm. She had to catch that train or she would be stuck for the night.

The city was packed with rush hour commuters. Police stopped people on the streets asking to see their passbooks. Letty walked down the avenue eyeing the *gendarmes*, but it was easy to blend into the metropolitan landscape and Letty soaked up the sights of people sipping drinks in cafes and others running for buses. It was her first time to this city.

She didn't know where the restaurant was and walked for blocks unsure if she was going the right direction. "Where is this street?" she asked, showing a man the address. He didn't want to stop and shrugged his shoulders. When a person did look at the address written on the paper, the old woman thought the street was back the way she came about twenty minutes.

A half-hour later she found the street and then the restaurant with a small, chipped sign that said, "Patisserie." She reached for the door and tugged at the handle. It was locked. No one was there. She knocked and no one came. "Where are these people?" She pounded on the door. It was silent. Letty didn't want to wait too long and miss the train, but she also had to make the delivery. She banged on the door one more time.

"Go away!" a gruff voice said inside. "We're closed."

"I have a package," she said. It was quiet again.

"Who's it for?" the voice said.

"I don't know."

"What is it?" the voice said through the door.

"I don't know. Can I show it to you?" It was quiet and she was impatient to get back to the train station. "There's a stamp with a rooster on it."

The door unlatched and opened revealing a large man towering above her. There was a scar on his forehead just above his eyebrow and his dark collared shirt was sweaty from the heat of the city.

"Let me see the package. Who are you?"

She didn't answer and held the package out for him to see the stamp.

"Come in," he said. "Have some food before you go." It was tempting, but something told her it was a bad idea.

"I just ate," she said. "Thank you."

"Girl, come in. I need to check to the contents of the package." It was a command, not a question anymore. She looked around the street. There was no one on this hidden side street, and even less in the confines of that dim restaurant with cigarette smoke wafting out.

"I really must go. I was told to drop a package here. That's all I know. I'm going to leave it with you." She set it down not taking her eyes off him and staying just out of his reach, then backed away before turning down the street. The man lifted the bag and started tearing at butcher paper to inspect the contents. He watched her out of the corner of his eye.

Her heart beat fast and she resisted the urge to run. Letty looked back once, but then kept her gaze forward and her ears open for footsteps. She weaved back through the side streets by the barred windows and shutters of stucco buildings weathered by the sea air. The walled roads wound forever.

She hung close to the cafes and shops to avoid detection watching the ground and the cracks in the road, and merged with the people on the streets as they ambled to their destinations. Towards the end of the block and the next intersection she saw a policeman observing people as they went by. His cylinder hat poked above the crowd as a warning sign.

Just beyond the policeman a small car pulled to the intersection. Her breath sucked in when she saw the ogre of a man from the restaurant sticking his head out the passenger side of a small Peugeot. He cranked his neck looking for her at the intersection while another man drove. Before she was able to duck into a store he spotted her and pointed.

Between them stood the policeman. She made a snap decision. Instead of running back the way she came she approached the *gendarmes*.

"Excuse me, officer!"

"Yes, Madame?"

"These Jewish men in that car are following me." It was the one thing she knew that might motivate the officer to act. "I feel unsafe."

"This car right here?" he said, pulling a notebook out of his pocket.

When Josiah's mafia contact saw her talking to the *gendarmerie* and pointing at him he barked at the driver who spun the steering wheel and sped away into the oncoming traffic.

"You see!" she said. "They drove away."

"I didn't get a clear view," he said. "Do you know them?"

"I don't," Letty said. "But they were making crude advances towards me. Thank you for your protection." She smiled, and started walking away up the street.

"Hold on, Madame. Where are you going? I need your paperwork please?" For my report. I need your name and a description."

"Oh sure," she said turning back to face him. "But I left my bag at home. I'm going now to fetch it."

"You left it at home?" he asked. "Your name please." He readied his pencil in his notebook.

"Letty," she said. "Letty Piccard." She read the name, Auguste Piccard, once in a book about hot-air balloons and it stuck in her mind. He was an inventor that broke the altitude records.

"Your address please," he said. The only address she knew was the one of the restaurant she just came from.

"11 Rue Lautard, next to a small Bistro," she said.

"That's very near here," he said. "I patrol this section of the city most days. If you ever need anything, Madame Piccard. Or if you see these men. Please notify me."

"Thank you." She walked towards the train station.

"Madame Piccard," he said. "Are you forgetting something?"

"Oh, yes. My bag. Thank you. Shall I bring my paperwork back for you?"

"It's okay this time, but you must keep it with you."

Letty circled through the neighborhood costing her time and back around the block scanning for the *mafioso* and the policeman before going toward the station.

The train's steam billowed out from the engine and over the tracks as Letty pushed through the station doors. She ran for her platform and grabbed the side of a passenger car pulling herself up the stairs as the train left for Montauban.

Josiah wasn't waiting when she arrived back hours later. It was late and the town was empty. Letty strolled over the red brick bridge leading out of the heart of the city towards the old part of town. Mother, Annie and Letty rented a room in a stone building on the river.

She pulled open the heavy door of the old tavern and took a ladder down into the rock cellar where mother and Annie were asleep. It never was meant for people, but Annie and Letty cleaned the rock floors and walls. It faced the river on one side and the other had a window chiseled through that was at ground level, letting in swarms of beetles, ants, and mice. The creepy crawlers combed through their things for crumbs. Something crunched under her feet (a beetle) as she stepped around the heavy breathing of Annie and bumped her head on the baskets of turnips and potatoes hanging from the ceiling. That's how they kept food safe from the infestation.

"Where have you been?" mother said in the darkness.

"I made a delivery to Marseille," she said. "I got us 1000 francs for it."

"Give it here," mother said. Letty gave her the crumpled bills as she lay in the pitch-blackness. Letty's eyes made out mother's shape lying in a makeshift bed in the dank room. She rustled around and the 500 francs were hidden away. "This doesn't feel like a 1000."

"I'm still owed 500."

Mother said nothing more. She didn't want the details. Letty brushed off her jacket that she used for a pillow, shook her blanket to be sure no bugs crawled in the bed, and closed her eyes.

35

Adapt, if you can.

Montech, France

"Josiah left in hurry," Leah said. "He packed his bags and told father that if anyone came asking for him, 'he was in Nice.'"

"Why?" Letty said. It made sense now why the mafia guy was after her.

"I don't know," she said.

"I'm not going to get the rest of the money?"

"He's gone."

When Letty returned from the egg deliveries there was a piece of paper tacked onto the door of the old stone building where they stayed. She thought it was from Josiah. It wasn't.

"*Résidence forcée.*"

She tore it down and read it. "All Jews are to be moved outside the city of Montauban to Montech," it said. There was nothing but farmland with miles of orchards in those parts. "By order of the Vichy government, you are assigned work on farmland."

Mother paced in the little stone cave pulling at her fingers and twisting her hair. The constant change was hard for her. She no longer was able to rationalize all the disruption in her life.

"We should have stayed in Lourdes!" she said on the verge of tears. "Annie, you said it was safe here. It was nice in Lourdes. And we were safe there. Now this! I don't know how to work on a farm. I'm too old to work on a farm."

"It will be okay, mother," Letty said.

"Oh, no. Don't give me that. Not you! Not you, the one who had me ride with that man and almost got us stranded!"

"We'll figure it out," Annie said. "We can do your work."

Police loaded them up in trucks in the city-center and drove into the country. Not knowing where they were going was the hardest part for mother. The truck shook as they passed the checkered fields of tilled crops and rows of orchards. Winter was approaching and it was a damp cold that stuck in your bones. The truck, only covered with a canvas top, screeched to a stop in front of a 300-year-old stone house. A policeman looked into the back of the truck and pointed at Letty.

"You," he said. "This is where you get off." They grabbed their suitcases and slung them to the ground and climbed out. Letty dragged their things into the house's courtyard and they waited like orphans as he knocked on the door of the house. A slight old woman dressed in black opened the door. Letty didn't hear what was said, but saw the policeman nod at them. Her face was neither welcoming nor hostile, but Letty gathered it wasn't her choice to have them.

Their room was two floors up and water was drawn from a pump downstairs. The toilet was in an outhouse twenty feet from the main cottage near the courtyard and was no more than a dirt hole dug into the ground.

"Why do you need so much water?" the old woman complained when Letty pumped the spigot into a bucket.

"We need to wash ourselves and our hair," Letty said looking at her suspicious face. She didn't like that they used so much of her water. If she could limit the air they breathed, she would have done so. The locals didn't like outsiders, but a horde of Jews in a time of war and economic distress was pushing any goodwill they had to the brink.

"I've never washed my hair," she said. "You could catch your death washing your hair." She had long silver hair and Letty noticed a grease stain that spread around the back of her dark dress.

She required Annie and Letty to give their food rations to her, which she divvied up as she saw fit. There was not much food to go around and hunger started in the belly and moved to the mind. It was all Letty thought about.

Letty called her Mrs. Stone. Not only did she look as if she crawled out of a rock, but she could squeeze water from a stone. She knew how much rations they were given and leaned in inspecting the milk and grain. "Don't try to play any tricks on me," she said. "I'm old, but I will know and so will the police."

Each time Letty brought water to mother the old woman reminded her of how much they used and warned about catching death. There was some truth to her words because the house was frigid during the winter. There was a small pot-bellied stove in their room, but it hardly heated the air around it. Sitting by the stove for warmth didn't work because while one side felt the warm glow, the other side became frozen. Instead, the three of them slept in a bed built into an alcove and huddled together for body heat. Letty grabbed bricks and set them on the stove to warm and put them under the covers. They laid together clinging to each other and the hot bricks.

Mother was a prisoner in the room, and Letty suffered more for her than for herself. Letty read her religious stories in Hebrew and Blima listened and moaned.

"I will not survive this," mother said. "The winter will kill me."

"Don't say these things," Letty said.

"It will."

36

Threats rise all around when you are tired.

When spring came, Letty and Leah (the Lerners were also relocated) found work collecting eggs in Montech to send to the city. They weren't paid much, but it was something. It was enough to get extra food for Blima.

"Josiah came back," Leah said while they carried the eggs in their aprons. "I heard him say he fled because of a deal gone wrong."

"What do you mean?"

"The delivery you made was for gold. But it wasn't exactly gold. It was actually lead dipped in a thin layer of gold."

"Fake gold?" A knot formed in Letty's stomach.

"The *Mafioso* is looking for you. He thinks you're the one that duped him!"

"Me?"

"When they found Josiah he told them it was you that switched the bars." The color drained from Letty's face. "They won't ever find you. Not in this war. It's all a mess. He told them you went to Paris with the gold to sell it to the Nazis."

"So now I'm being hunted by the mafia?" It seemed too crazy to believe that Josiah duped the Jewish mob and let her take the fall. But she trusted Leah and knew it was probably true.

"The *gendarmes* are after all Jews. The mafia will never catch you. They don't even know your name." Letty wasn't so sure and went silent and stared into the canal with sycamore trees and plowed fields on one side and orchards on the other. As much as it worried her, she had more pressing things to focus on. The picking season was about to start per the terms of France's forced labor of Jews.

When the light crept over the horizon Letty and Annie arrived at the orchard the next day, a few miles from the stone house where they stayed. Mr. Kayser, the "walking boss" from Luxembourg, handed them baskets.

"You will fill seventy of these each day," he said. "Now get to it. You, brownies," he said to the Spaniards. "Get your lazy butts over here and start picking. This town supports you and you think you get a free ride. Let's go!" There were two other girls, refugees from Spain. They had trouble understanding his French and his frustration with them was apparent as he tossed baskets at their feet.

Letty started for the nearest tree with the basket and reached up picking the low hanging fruit.

"Not those!" he yelled at her. "Get a ladder." He walked around them holding a whip and snarling in French and German. "Don't even think about eating those peaches. You're here to pick them, not eat them." The girls were so hungry, the thought did cross the mind. He smacked the whip against his tall boots. "You're picking them all wrong. Don't pull the fruit. You'll bruise it! Tip the peach sideways like this." He came up near Letty and she smelled his foul, dung breath. "Give it a light twist and it will release from the branch without a bruise. Do not bruise the fruit! I repeat, do not bruise the fruit! If you choose not to pick them right, I will send you to the internment camps. You think it's hard here? Just wait."

After four hours Letty's back and calves ached from going on her tiptoes and she was sweating through her dress in the summer heat. Her stomach growled with hunger. She wanted to eat one of those peaches. The smell of the fruit wafted into her nose and then tore at her stomach. Annie was picking the tree next to her and moved like a machine. Mr. Kayser snapped his whip near Letty, "I want 70 baskets from you! You're lagging. I only count thirty. Are you stupid? Do you not know how to count?"

He walked up to Letty and stopped. She kept picking and thought about her technique while his scrutiny made her hand shake. He tapped his whip against his leg. "You're bruising the fruit! How can I count a bruised fruit? I'm going to check every one of your peaches."

Mr. Kayser cracked his whip again and again. "Speed up!" he yelled. "We don't have all day!"

Letty wound her way up and down two rows of fruit trees and had picked 70 baskets of peaches by days end. She hefted the heavy baskets to Mr. Kayser's flatbed truck where he tallied her haul. "70," he said. "Now we need to look at your fruit. You ruined more peaches than you picked."

Annie waited for her as Mr. Kayser inspected the fruit. "You get a move on," he said. "Your sister is going to be here a while." He pulled out every fruit that he said was bruised and tossed it into a spoils pile. Letty waved Annie on and she left towards the house. "Now by my count you need another six baskets after I pulled out the fruit you bruised. Get picking."

It took her the better part of an hour, but she picked him six more baskets. He leaned against his truck the entire time tapping his whip against his thigh. "I hope you've learned one thing today. Don't bruise the fruit."

She lumbered back along the road picking up one foot and putting it in front of the other. The stone house was still two miles away. Darkness was coming and cars rumbled by. About a half mile up the rode a rusted car with chipped paint pulled up and a man leaned over. He was wearing a shirt that was dusty from working in one of the orchards.

"I'm heading a few miles up," he said. "You need a ride?" She was tired and didn't have much left in her for the rest of the way.

"Sure," Letty said. "Thanks." He reached over and unlocked the door and she slid into the seat not thinking whether it was appropriate of her to accept a ride from a strange man. Her tired body and mind weren't functioning.

"Where are you going?" he said.

"I'm at the stone house in a mile." He drove not saying anything else, but glancing over to her. He veered off the road before they reached the house down a dirt road into a nearby field.

"This is the wrong way," Letty said. "It's up there!"

"Don't worry. It's a short cut."

"What are you saying?" she said. Before she knew what he was getting at he stopped the car and reached over sticking his hand between her legs. The rough calluses of his hands scratched through her dress.

"This field is a good place for us."

"Get off me!"

"Don't worry," he said. "No one will see us. This is what you wanted."

"Stop!" But he was already pulling her dress up over her knees. The sun got lower in the sky. She pushed her dress back down with one hand and tugged at his hand between her legs with the other while he kissed at her neck.

"This is the way you like it." Oil stuck to his fingers as they wrapped around her throat and collarbone pinning her back. He undid his pants. He smelled of cigarettes, sweat, and gasoline. She was having trouble breathing. His face was a blurry mess of hair and stubble. Letty was stuck in slow motion, and his thin cracking lips came for her. She saw the animal in his black eyes. It was a swirl of chaos before she realized that not only was he going to rape her, but do something even worse, as his fingers tightened around her neck.

She wiggled and twisted, but the harder she resisted and tried to break free the more he tightened his grip, and bore down with his weight. Her entire body was flooded with dread. Then, her mind cleared.

With her free hand she scratched at his throat forcing him to take his hand off her neck, and in the split second she felt his grip release Letty thrust her forehead with all her force into his face smashing his nose. He fell back cursing and clasping his nasal region with both hands. She took her free leg and kicked him in the chest. He reached for Letty again and she kicked. She grasped to open the door feeling it click and tumbled out onto the dirt, rolling face down, and dragged herself from the car, digging her fingers into the earth. Her feet moved underneath her and in seconds she raced into the field. She heard him yell, but then there was only her breathing as she ran, her lungs bursting in pain. She didn't dare stop.

Letty was back at the house in minutes, but waited a half hour to gather herself before going inside. She pumped some water from the spigot as Mrs. Stone watched. She lugged the splashing pail upstairs.

"What's this blood?" mother said. She sat in bed covered in blankets, even though it was warm outside. On Letty's dress were sprays of blood and her face too.

"Someone was hit in the nose with a branch while picking," she said. "I helped them clean up."

"You have scratches on your face and neck."

"The peach trees."

Letty didn't tell her, or anyone about the assault. There was enough else to worry about. The stress might have pushed mother over the edge. There was no point and nothing to be done. They were already a burden to the police, and the local people despised them.

She got up the next morning like nothing happened and headed up the same road back to the orchard where Mr. Kayser gave her baskets to fill. He stood watching her pick, tapping the whip against his palm. Her fingers didn't shake as she pulled the peaches from the tree. He said nothing and moved to the Spanish girls. "You brownies are the worst! 70 baskets. I'll wait all night for you to give 70 perfect baskets."

For six weeks Annie and Letty reported to the orchard. Mother stayed at the stone house complaining about the outhouse and how Mrs. Stone watched her like a thief. The language barrier and mother's persistence at lighting candles and abiding by her religious customs didn't help ease the suspicions of the woman, or relieve mother's discomfort. It was harder for mother to find the Orthodox women of Antwerp she had enjoyed in Luchon and Lourdes, in this rural town. Instead she paced the room during the day like a prison cell, while Mr. Kayser swung his whip in the orchard demanding Annie and Letty to pick faster.

There were only four pickers in Letty's section of the orchard, but as she saw the trees bare of fruit, relief set in. There was an end in sight to the crack of Mr. Kayser's whip and the spitting of his harsh words. She dropped the last basket of peaches in front of him for the day and he tallied it. Annie followed behind lugging hers to the tree he sat under for shade. Their faces were dark and peeling from the sun.

"Toby and I are going to swim at the canal today," she said to Letty. "Do you want to come? I'm learning to swim."

Letty agreed. She still didn't know how to swim, but also didn't want to walk home alone. They met Toby at a junction in the farmlands and cut through a thicket of brush and a field of barley to the canal, which syphoned water from the Garonne River. There was a little grassy knoll, and it was a hot day, but rows of trees kept them shaded. Toby knew how to swim and jumped in. Annie slid in and pushed her hands through the flowing water swimming like a bobbing cat.

"Why don't you come in?" Toby said. "Do you know how to swim?" Letty dragged her toes in the water and thought of the lake and the waterfall in the snow-capped Pyrenees and Theo. Back then, she wished she knew how to swim.

Toby climbed out of the steep canal ledge, dripping, and her white undergarments clung to her. "Don't be scared, Letty," she said. "Do you know the best way to learn to swim? I can show you if you want. It's very simple." She was calm and helpful.

"No, what is it?" Letty said. She felt Toby's hand on her back and then she was falling into the canal encased in the cool water in an instant. She sank and water rushed up her nose and mouth,

151

the pressure stinging her nasal cavity. She gulped and water filled her lungs. She swung her arms thrashing to keep herself above the waterline.

"Letty, move your arms against the water!" Annie said. She was too far away and not much of a swimmer to help, and Toby just laughed at her desperate slaps at the water. Letty's dress pulled her down and she fought it gasping for air.

"Help! Help!" she screamed when her mouth touched the surface. Toby stood at the steep edge of the canal amused by the whites of her eyes and the frantic pleas. Perhaps she was getting her back for the office fiasco at Behr's, which claimed her job.

The fear of death washed over Letty. Then her arms paddled like a dog and she moved through the water, no longer dropping to the bottom. She chopped her way to the edge and strained to pull herself out of the water with every muscle drained. Annie gave her a push and she landed in the safety of the tall grass, her hair stuck to her face, and sprawled out. She looked through her hair over at Toby who thought the whole thing was a fun joke.

"Letty, you learned to swim," she said. "I guess you owe me."

37

Beware of bigger things (like the sudden change of a law).

While Letty was learning to swim with Toby and Annie, Pierre Laval was reassuming power as the head of the Vichy government in 1942. He was Marshal Pétain's number one advisor. The Vichy newspapers heralded his ascension, but for Jewish refugees it was that moment when the bad got worse. Letty and her family knew little of international events like Hitler's invasion of Russia or Pearl Harbor, but they felt the escalation of the Vichy's crackdown on the Jews. There was little hope except for a few BBC news radio reports Annie heard that said the British were winning key battles, otherwise it was only Vichy propaganda and anti-Jewish broadcasts.

When the Nazis opened a front against the Russians, they were all of sudden short skilled labor. Hitler demanded 300,000 workers from France. A deal was cut: For every three workers France sent to Germany, they received in return one French prisoner of war. Heinrich Himmler, the head of the Nazi Gestapo, at the same time pressured Laval to round up every Jew in France and send them to German-occupied Poland.[1]

A light bulb went off for Laval, and he had an idea that killed two birds with one stone. He went after all Jewish refugees, foreign Jews like Letty, for immediate deportation to the Germans. Laval even went outside the terms stipulated by the Nazis and sent children under 16, whom the Germans said he could spare. He didn't want to break up families.[2]

Because of the Vichy's new deal to send foreign Jews to Germany the *razzias* became more frequent and intense. Rene Bousquet, the head of French police and the Nazi SS created a plan to round up all foreign Jews. Police were ordered to check travel documents at bus and train stations, and they cordoned off neighborhoods, going house-to-house searching for Jews.[3]

Of course rumors of a police list in Montech for a round up circulated the grapevine like wildfire. They were going to arrest every Jew and send them to the internment camp, Drancy. Letty, Annie and her mother didn't have a travel pass and if the rumors were true, they were stuck.

Annie and Letty wandered through the small town in the late afternoon trying to get more information from other Jewish refugees. The rumor of the list had all the Jews on edge and the streets were filled only with local French farmers. On the corner was a local *gendarme*, patrolling, and Annie and Letty's first instinct was that this man was going to stop them and ask for papers.

He looked at them, but instead of a mistrustful stare he gave a warm smile and a wave from across the street. His hair was greying underneath the cylinder cap, and the leather straps holding his gear that crossed his wide belly were stretched from the years. Though his blue uniform was clean, it was well-worn and faded.

"Annie, let's ask this policeman about the list," Letty said.

"That's a bad idea."

"If he was going to arrest us he wouldn't have waved." Letty crossed the empty street in front of Annie who didn't follow. The policeman strolled by a butcher shop and was about to cross over to the next street.

"Pardon, officer," she said turning her French accent up. He stopped and faced her.

"How can I help you, Madame?" he said.

"My sister and I have been picking peaches in the orchards for a farmer," Letty said. "We've heard rumors that there are lists of people that are going to be picked up and moved. Is that true?" He scanned her face for clues.

"I tell you what, if you walk over to the station with me I'll check for you."

Letty's heart beat fast, but they had no choice except to follow or run. Annie stared at Letty angry at her reckless idea. They strolled with him to the small station down the street and he opened the door, letting them enter first. He followed them inside and went to a desk, picking up his paperwork, putting on reading spectacles, and then waved them over.

"So indeed, we have received orders from the General Secretary of Police, Bousquet." He removed the spectacles. "There's a list. What's the last name and I'll check to see if you're on it?" They looked at each other like they didn't know if they should give their true names. He could arrest them right then. It was too late, but they had to know.

"Last name is Schmidt," Annie said. "Annie and Letty Schmidt." He put his specs back on and scanned the papers with his finger.

"Yes, you're on the list along with a Blima Schmidt." Their skin prickled and Annie shuddered at the mention of mother's name. He kept looking over his paperwork and he took his glasses off again. "We'll be coming." He stared at them making sure they understood what he was saying.

He put his glasses back on and started writing out paperwork. It was about ten minutes with him writing and saying nothing to them. Letty's mind raced as to what he was doing. Was he writing arrest papers? At last he shuffled the papers together and took his glasses off one final time. He handed Annie the paperwork, but didn't say what it was before he showed them out the door.

When the policeman walked back into the station they sped up to a brisk pace heading towards the stone farmhouse. Annie then stopped to look over the papers the policeman gave her.

"C'mon, we need to go," Letty said.

"These are travel passes for you, mother, and me," she said and handed them to Letty. "I'm going to warn Toby and the Lerners." She headed towards where the Lerners stayed and called back over her shoulder. "Start packing and get mother's things together."

Letty arrived at the house and mother was pacing the room. "What did you find out?" she said.

"We need to leave Montech now." Mother didn't ask any questions. She had heard the rumors and now Letty confirmed them.

"Why didn't Annie come back with you?"

"She went to warn the Lerners."

"She's putting us at risk. Causing confusion."

Annie was only a half-hour later than Letty. They lugged their suitcases down the stairs, not saying goodbye to Mrs. Stone. Letty didn't know where she was and didn't care. Annie and Letty traded off carrying mother's suitcase to the bus station. When they went to buy the bus tickets the attendant asked for their identity cards. Letty gave them to him and mother gave Letty money for the tickets.

"I need to see your travel permits," he said. "Foreigners must have travel permits." Letty gave him the documents the policeman had just written an hour earlier. He looked them over and handed them back along with three tickets to Montauban. The importance of paperwork was that it allowed them to travel wherever they wanted in France. Before that policeman wrote out the passes, they were relegated to Montech.

"Can I see your documents for travel?" he said to mother. The bus attendant stared at mother who hovered nearby. She looked at him with a blank stare and then at her daughters not understanding.

"My mother is a mute and doesn't speak," Letty said. "I gave them to you already. Look, here they are." She showed the paperwork again pointing to her name and the policeman's signature. He nodded and waved his hand. Letty pulled mother away from the man and towards their bus.

The 8-mile drive to Montauban took twenty minutes, and there mother knew two Jewish women, named Gruber, from Strasbourg. She knocked on their door and the Grubers welcomed them with guarded, if not courteous, smiles.

It was a small room, but the Grubers let them stay, not fearing arrest themselves because they were French citizens. Mother threw her clothes around digging for something as she unpacked.

"I can't believe this happened!" she said. "We left all our money in Montech!"

"But mother, I saw you put your wallet in your jacket at the bus station," Letty said. "We paid for the tickets."

"No, no!" she put her hands on her head. The Grubers tried to relax her giving her warm tea. It was all of their money they earned; the money Letty got from Josiah, the money delivering eggs. Mother hid it inside the alarm clock from Antwerp. It sat like an innocuous timepiece high on a shelf and out of sight in Mrs. Stone's farmhouse. Mother had been stuffing bills in the space inside.

"I'll go back and get it," Letty said to calm her. Mother didn't argue.

Letty walked back to the bus station and caught a bus to Montech to retrieve the alarm clock. Her mind was on the *razzia* they were warned about. She didn't know when it was happening, but it was soon according to the policeman. When the bus arrived at the Montech terminal with a loud squeal, the station looked the same as when they left hours earlier. Desolate of people. She walked to the farmhouse in the evening air and the roads were empty except for blowing leaves and slinking cats. Dogs barked on farms in the distance.

At the front of the farmhouse a light was on in the kitchen where the old woman puttered. Letty opened the door without a squeak and climbed the three flights of stairs on the balls of her feet. It seemed the woman didn't even know they had left. The floors creaked no matter which board she stepped on. Then the door to their room groaned as she opened it. Up on the top shelf was the alarm clock. She used a chair to reach it careful not to thump the ground when she climbed off.

Letty held her breath going down the stairs tucking the alarm clock under her arm. She only had a little further to go and sneak by the kitchen. At the bottom, though, stood Mrs. Stone, illuminated by the kitchen's kerosene lamp. Her face was too dark to see but her skeleton flickered in the light. She lifted her finger pointing her gnarled nail at Letty.

"You!" she said. "Think I didn't notice you people sneaking out in the night?" Her voice cracked and echoed off the stone walls. "Like rats. What do you have there?"

"My mother's clock," she said.

"You're stealing my things!"

"We took nothing," she said. "It's my mother's."

"If you try to take my things the police will take you."

"You're mistaken," Letty said. There was no reasoning with her.

"I knew you were going to steal. I told them you were going to steal. A bunch of ungrateful foreigners. And now you are stealing. I knew it! Thieves! Leave it!" the old woman commanded. Letty stepped around her and the woman made a feeble grab at her.

"The police will be notified." She snatched her coat to put on as Letty went out the door. Letty's chest burned and beads of sweat formed at her temples.

At the bus station she studied the timetables and it was forty-five minutes until the next bus to Montauban. Sitting in a corner hidden from plain view she watched the time and scanned the door for the *gendarmes* and Mrs. Stone. Each time an elderly lady walked through the door her heart leaped. Just the sight of grey hair made her palms sweat. Scenarios played in her head of police pounding on the doors downtown with the vindictive woman chomping at their shoulders commanding them to search for the clock. Finding nothing, they might decide to swarm the bus station, hunting her down.

Then Letty saw a *gendarme* enter the station. It was her worst fear playing out. He was coming towards her like he was searching for someone.

"What are you doing, girl?" he said. This was it. Letty looked around for Mrs. Stone. "Papers."

She fished into the bag that hung around her neck and handed him the papers. He looked at it close and then at her. She expected him to take her in for stealing the alarm clock.

"Tomorrow I have to come and pick you people up. Do you understand?" He stared at her to see if what he said registered. "We are picking all Jews up and sending them to a camp."

"My mother and sister are in Montauban," I said. "You can pick me up if you want."

"Get out of here," he said handing her card back. "Leave Montech. You have a travel pass. I suggest you use it and go."

"I'm leaving. I have a ticket."

"Good. Don't come back."

Letty took her I.D. and travel documents from him. She thought, "how dumb for the cop to be telling me his plans and not arresting me on the spot." She watched him patrol the empty station looking down the hallways.

Her bus pulled in and Letty looked one more time for Mrs. Stone before boarding. She handed the driver a ticket and slid low into the seat peeking out the window. The driver tugged on a handle and the door closed. Letty had the alarm clock on her lap for mother.

[1] Warner, Geoffrey, *Pierre Laval and the Eclipse of France*, New York: The Macmillan Company, 1968, pp. 307–10, 364.

[2] Paldiel, Mordecai. *Churches and the Holocaust: Unholy Teaching, Good Samaritans, and Reconciliation*, p. 82.

[3] Cesarani, David. *The Final Solution: Origins and Implementation*, Routledge, 1994, p 198.

38

Good ideas may sound crazy at first.

Lourdes, France

The *razzias* spread from city to town to village under Bousquet and German SS Police Leader, Carl Oberg. Letty was afraid to show her face on the streets, but hiding was just as dangerous. Rumors about friends being dragged from closets and arrested spread. The more the Nazis needed laborers, the more their demand on the French to capture foreign Jews.

Bousquet's technique was to cordon off several blocks of a neighborhood and go house-to-house rooting out Jews. The first well-publicized one was in Paris. 13,000 Jews were arrested. When Catholic bishops protested, Bousquet threatened to close their schools.

"We can emigrate to Switzerland," Letty said.

"You with your stupid ideas," mother said.

"We aren't safe in France."

"We aren't safe anywhere. You want to run to Switzerland? Do you know where it is? How close Switzerland is to Germany? Where will we live? Will they let us in? Put us in camps? Think, Letty! You don't think! You're reckless." Saliva sprayed out of Blima's mouth, her words chopped and cut and her eyes, although fierce, were on the verge of tears. She was scared. "We're cast to these wretched lives. I had a nice house in Antwerp, and now I don't even have a bed. This is a miserable life. You think this is a fun adventure."

They spent two days with the Grubers in Montauban, but their welcome was wearing out. The Grubers didn't want trouble with the police and "to be seen as harboring foreign Jews."

"Suzy is in Lourdes," mother said. "We'll go there. She'll know what to do. Rebecca and Elijah are there too. He's smart and has good ideas." They were the young couple Blima trusted more than her young daughters. Mother's eyes were wild and flitting around the room unable to focus on any one spot. She wasn't able to make sound decisions, and there was no reasoning with her. But her daughters followed her wishes to be near Suzy and her good friends.

When they arrived back in Lourdes, Letty left Suzy a note at the last known address they had for her, which was a nice hotel. During the war hotels were converted into refugee housing and were easy targets for Bousquet to conduct *razzias,* sending the Jews who lived there to internment camps. Lourdes, however, didn't cooperate with him like other cities and provinces.

It was two weeks before Suzy answered Letty's message. She arrived wearing a dress fitted just for her and red lipstick. Her real family must have appeared like peasants in their stained dresses by comparison.

"I've missed you, Suzy!" mother said. "How have you been?"

"The Richfelds are taking good care of me."

Mother was silent, but her face twitched at Suzy's words.

"Are you here for help?" Suzy asked. She looked at them gauging their reaction. "I don't think we can help you. Times are tough for all of us. You know how it is."

Silence fell on the room and all eyes were on Suzy tapping the wall with her fingernails. They were filed and polished. Her patent leather short heels shined.

"Do you have any plans?" Suzy said.

"I think Switzerland is an option," Letty said. She didn't want Suzy to think they were here for her help.

"Letty, forget that stupid idea," mother said. Suzy looked at Letty and the wheels turned in her head. A little grin curled up on Letty's lips. That was the reaction she wanted.

"I'm going to Marseille tomorrow," Annie said. "Toby wrote that she has a job in a school outside of the city—"

Suzy didn't listen to Annie her eyes drifting to the window and her hands now clasped together, wringing out her boredom. Annie's voice trailed lower.

"I'm expected somewhere soon. Keep me informed about where you end up."

"We will, Suzy," mother said.

39

Don't count on dumb luck, but it does happen.

Marseille, France

A train rolled over the track, filling the void between Annie and Blima. Mother faced Annie and put her arms around her, squeezing tight. Annie put her arms around mother, holding her. She breathed in her scent, not wanting to forget. Not one word was spoken, but that was okay. Annie dropped her arms and wiped her eyes. Mother let go and Annie saw she had tears too. Something about the moment felt final to Annie.

She picked up her suitcase and stepped up the stairs of the train and found a seat by the window. She saw mother standing and waved. Mother waved back, and wiped her nose. The train pulled away and Annie watched mother until she was just a spec on the train platform and then gone.

The train twisted its way towards the coast stopping at stations. Police filed through the cars staring at faces, but Annie focused on the switch house outside the window. Her thoughts of mother disappeared as did her worries about the *gendarmerie*. She climbed down the train's stairs in Marseille and pushed through the crowd of travelers running for trains.

The sea breeze was a cool repose, but the hot sun of the day still radiated off the walls and cement. Annie found the three-story building, its windows with shutters all closed in the late day. She knocked and it opened a crack and an old man poked through the door. It was a rooming house for Jewish refugees.

"I am here to see the Lerners," she said. "They have a room." The man let her pass with no questions. In the maze of winding stairs and hallways of the old building Annie became lost. By chance she saw Dora Lerner climbing a staircase with a basket of wash to hang out the window.

Mrs. Lerner put her pile of clothes down and hugged Annie and led her through the snaking halls. Their room was small, with two twin cots and a window shutter that opened into the street. She gave Annie what little they had to eat: bread, a hard boiled egg, and boiled carrots.

"You're joining Toby at the school?" Mrs. Lerner asked Annie. The school was located on the outskirts of Marseille.

"My children are spread all over this country thanks to the Vichy," Mr. Lerner said. "Josiah comes in and out. He brings us food, though. A good kid. Smart, industrious and good-looking. However, Chayim is going to be a rabbi. His studies of the Torah are extensive. He'll be a rabbi one day. Mark my words. And you know, Toby is a very smart for a girl."

Outside there was a screeching of wheels. Mr. Lerner ignored the noise and gushed about his children while Annie sat with her hands folded listening. Annie heard more wheels squeaking and car doors slammed. She looked at the window. There was now yelling and pounding on doors. Mr. Lerner ignored the noises outside and told Annie about Chayim's "wonderful" reading of the Torah for his bar mitzvah last year. "His voice radiated with meaning! He will be a rabbi!" Annie remembered the joke the boy said during Purim and how bad she felt for smiling at its ill humor.

On the other side of the Lerners' door people ran through the hallways slamming doors. Mr. Lerner, who was about 70, at last took notice of the commotion. Mrs. Lerner stood by the window cracking the shutters.

"What's going on?" he said.

"It's a *razzia!*" she said. "The *gendarmerie* cars are blocking the streets. Police are running from building to building!" She slid against the wall away from the window. Mr. Lerner pushed up from the chair and limped to the window to see for himself.

"Oh my!" he gasped. "Oh my! A woman jumped from a third-story window trying to escape! They're pulling her off the street. Dragging her body." He moved from the window, his hand covering his mouth. Annie saw the fear in their eyes. She didn't know what to do. They were coming for them.

"Quick!" Mrs. Lerner said. "Annie, under the bed now! I'll lay over you."

"No, Mrs. Lerner," Annie said. "I can't let you risk yourself!"

"Big trucks are pulling up outside and more *gendarmes* are coming," Mr. Lerner said, peeking out. Annie heard the rumble of the engines and squeal of breaks. It was now dark and only the street lamps cast yellow light on the police breaking into the houses as they threw their shoulders into doors.

"Get under the bed," she said pushing Annie towards a cot. Annie climbed beneath and lay listening to the quick beats of her heart. Mrs. Lerner crawled into the bed and threw the covers over herself, and Annie felt the mattress press against her above and the cold wood floor below. She looked at the dust on the planks and the rusted nail heads, and kept her ear pressed to the ground. She didn't dare move, and heard a fist pounding on the building's main door. The beating reverberated in the boards against her ear. She stopped breathing to listen. Mr. Lerner switched the lights off. Now only the light from under the door was seen. She heard boots running through the hallways inside the building. Loud bangs echoed off the stucco walls. "Open up!" loud voices demanded in French. Doors were broke open and shrieks and then shuffling of bare feet being dragged. "Noooo!

Please! My children!" Screams pleaded down the hallway. Annie waited for their turn. She knew there was nothing to be done as the arrests proceeded. She saw the heels of boots stomp by in the crack under the door and heard the jingling of metal, perhaps keys, handcuffs, or a Billy club. More yells and then crying from a room down the hallway as the boots stomped back by with more bare feet sliding. "My family!" a woman cried. "We have done nothing!" It went on for an eternity. Annie lay motionless, closing her eyes, knowing they must be next. With every stomp of boots Annie braced for her turn.

Big trucks out front revved their engines, filling the night air with exhaust and headlight beams, which reflected into the room. There were a few faint yells on the street and the crowded trucks grumbled with the extra weight, shaking the shutters, but then there was nothing but stillness outside and in the building. Not a peep. Annie didn't dare move, listening for anything. It was the beauty of silent nothingness. Her mind withdrew into the abyss and she opened her eyes as someone does from a nightmare, sucking deep for air and life. But this wasn't a dream and Annie was still lying there by either luck or divine intervention.

40

There's a big difference between proactive problem-solving, and wishful thinking.

Lourdes, France

"Elijah has an escape plan," mother said. "He's very clever." She didn't say what the plan was, just that "he has it figured out." It was a middle-aged couple mother grew to trust with her life. They ate, reminisced about Antwerp, discussed the war, and celebrated Simchat Torah and other Jewish holidays together. Above all, mother wanted to believe someone had the answer, and she was certain Letty didn't.

"Have you heard about Switzerland?" Letty asked Elijah and Rebecca in the lobby hotel while they sat with Blima.

"I've heard it's possible," Elijah said. Mother twisted her napkin so tight her knuckles became white and her lips tightened to a perfect straight line. "But I confess I don't know where you go."

"Stop your foolishness," mother said, glaring at Letty. "You're just looking for excuses to gallivant. Leave them alone with your questions." Her stare softened when she turned to Elijah, whose thick, kinky, brown hair was combed to the side. "She's impulsive. Selfish really. Please excuse her."

The Bishop in Lourdes was protecting Jews, but it was a matter of time before France closed off all exits for foreign Jews. They were circling them like a pack of hunting dogs and you had to be stupid or too scared not to notice.

One day Letty saw a newspaper sitting on a table through the window in a patisserie. She went in and thumbed through it for information on the war. She knew it was Vichy propaganda, but it was all they had.

"Are you going to pay for that?" a man's voice said from behind her.

"Sorry, I thought it was rubbish," she said. Letty set it down and turned to leave.

"Relax, it was a joke," the man said before she walked out. "Have a seat. Let me treat you to a drink." Letty looked up and a good-looking gentleman in a suit and tie, older than her by about twenty years, stood smiling. If she refused she might draw suspicion. Plus, saying "no" to a free glass of wine was stupid.

"Thank you," she said. She avoided eye contact and blood rushed to her cheeks.

"What's your name?" he said.

"Letty."

"I'm Nicholas. Your accent sounds like you're from the north?"

"I am. North of Paris."

"I know Paris well. It's much further north than Paris." Letty said nothing and sipped the wine he brought to the table. It was sweet on her lips and dry in her mouth as she swished it over her tongue letting it slide down. "Do you like Lourdes?" he asked.

She nodded yes.

"You don't say much. You're shy."

"I don't know you," she said feeling the wine in her veins and holding the stem of the small glass.

"I run this restaurant. I hear a lot. And I see a lot." Letty became self-conscious and looked over her shoulder. The patisserie was empty. "Relax, I'm not trying to entrap you, but I can tell you're a traveler."

"Why do you say that?"

"Your clothes, your hair, the roughness of your hands," he said. She winced at his words. "Don't get me wrong, you're very pretty. If I had to guess I'd say you were forced to work on a farm recently."

"You gathered all that from my appearance?" she said, drinking the rest of the wine. "Thank you for the drink. I need to be going." Letty didn't like the game he was playing.

"If I owned this placed I would have to register it with the Vichy because I'm a Jew," he said. "I also read the newspapers and know about the forced work on farms." She nodded, acknowledging he was right.

"What will they do to Jewish businesses?"

"Depends. They could take them away. 'Aryanize' them as they say." He swished his wine glass. "Where you from?"

"Antwerp."

"Never been. Is it nice? You're pretty." Her face became hot from the wine and the compliment.

"Have you heard about Switzerland?" she said.

"Where did they have you working?"

"Montech."

"Was it bad?"

Letty shrugged.

"Picking peaches was horrible only because the overseer was cruel."

"You poor girl. How could they treat such a pretty girl so bad? Did you escape?"

"We finished the picking." A person walked into the patisserie and Nicholas stood up. The last of the sun was glowing in the sky and its rays fought through the cracks of buildings.

"Hello, *Monsieur*," Nicholas said. "What can I get you?" The patron looked over at Letty.

"A baguette," the man said. Nicholas handed it over and the man went away.

"What about Switzerland? It is possible to cross?" Letty asked.

"Yes. I know people that have made it there. Would you like to come home with me?" His eyes were dark, kind, and desperate, but hopeful.

She smiled at his boldness and then giggled to herself.

"Every time I tell my mother she tells me to forget Switzerland. It's a 'stupid idea' she tells me."

"I'd say its one of the best options there is. You have to be careful, but as far as I can see, there is not much else." He leaned back in his wooden chair across the round, metal table from Letty.

"You could show me how to do it so I don't get hurt," she said. Letty looked down at her empty wine glass and her stomach fluttered.

"Pardon me, Madame," Nicholas said. "Let me refill your glass." He got up and poured the glass full to the top.

"If I wanted to cross into Switzerland, where do I go?"

He disappeared into the back of the restaurant behind the counter and brought back a book. In the book was a map and he pointed to a spot.

"I've heard this is where smugglers like to leave from," he said.

Letty read the spot on the map he pointed to; "Annemasse." It was a few miles from Geneva, and a few days trip from where they sat now in Lourdes. A little piece of Switzerland jetted out like a finger into France beckoning her.

"Is Switzerland really safer than France?"

"Safer than the Vichy?" he said. "Yes. From what I hear the Nazis leave the Swiss alone. Their generals and colonels like to take leave there, and Hitler hides money there."

Letty studied the map not wanting to forget the crossing spot.

"You need fake papers so you can travel. I know a guy that can get you the documents."

"Here in Lourdes?"

"Oh, no. Marseille. Let me see your hands?" Letty gave him her left hand. He took it running his fingers over her palm and the calluses and cuts. "Even with all the work your hands are nice. I love your hands. They are small."

He kneaded his fingers into her hand and the tingles from his touch released the tension in her mind and muscles better than the wine.

She felt a deep relaxation from her head to the tips of her fingers and toes, and warm blood started flowing in her chest. She closed her eyes and his hands moved up her arm. Not wanting him to stop, she let him go on. Letty never felt a touch like that. He stood up over her and rubbed his hands into her shoulders and then teased them over her collarbone sliding them just far enough.

"Come back to my house," Nicholas said.

"Okay." It was so easy to say yes.

He got up to close the shop letting her sink into the chair where she came back to her senses. Mother was at their room. She stood up arranging her dress.

"You look beautiful," he said. "Are you ready?"

She hugged his chest burying her face into his jacket. She felt safe. His arms folded around her back and squeezed tight. Tears flowed down her cheeks in the arms of this stranger. She looked up at him and his dark eyes. His dark hair was combed back with care, and there were greys around his ears.

"Why are you crying sweet girl? What have I done?"

She pressed up and kissed him on the lips. He pulled her closer lifting her up and then set her down. His hands wiped her tears. He looked at her trying to read her face. There was no way for him to know. Her longing for his embrace, the protection of his arms, and the impossibility of their situation was only the top layer.

"I must go. My mother is waiting for me."

"No," he said. "I won't let you. You're trapped here." She wished it were true.

Then he smiled and opened the door of the patisserie for her. She stepped out into the crisp air and felt refreshed.

"Hold on," he said. He went back into the shop and came out with a piece of paper. "Here's the name and address of the man who can help with paperwork." He said it real quiet so no one on the street could overhear.

Letty clutched it in her hand on the sly and kissed him on the cheek, feeling like she was in one of the Hitchcock spy movies she had watched in Antwerp.

41

When lambs protect lambs, the wolves will come.

Marseille, France

Bousquet and the Nazis' Carl Oberg ordered *razzias* throughout Marseille, sending thousands of Jews to internment camps. The police simply missed the Lerners' room in the winding network of stairs, hallways, and doors. It was true that the Lerners were too old for arrest according to Vichy orders from Pierre Laval, but Annie wasn't.

Annie hiked up the road outside Marseille covered by the swaying trees and saw the children chasing each other in the fields. Their parents were either already interned, deported to the camps, or in hiding. The children were left with a rabbi for protection and being under 16 years of age were not under direct threat of arrest. On the hill a spotter was posted to warn about approaching *gendarmes*. The schoolhouse sat in front of a mountain on the outskirts of the city at the end of a tree-lined road.

Rabbi Zalman Schneerson became a French resident years earlier when he moved from Russia with his wife, daughter and son—the only reason keeping him from being rounded up by the Vichy. He technically wasn't a foreign Jew.

"Someone approaches!" a voice yelled in the distance. The children ran up the hill disappearing behind the school into the mountain. The grass-covered hill was empty of people in a matter of seconds. In the distance a person stepped out of the building and came toward her. Annie squinted her eyes and saw it was Toby.

"Annie!" Toby said, her shout echoing. "I've missed you!" She threw her arms around her shy friend. "C'mon, I'll introduce you to Rabbi Schneerson."

The rabbi was surveying damage on a wall of the house. He pointed to rotting wood with another man that held a hammer and piece of wood siding. Even with Vichy persecution the rabbi wore his Hasidic dress: a wide brimmed hat, long red beard, curling side locks and spoke French in a strong Russian accent. He was tall, thin and wore a black suit. He hobbled up to Annie on his clubfoot to welcome her with a smile.

"There's food inside, warm clothes, and a shower," he said. "Toby will show you around. You'll help her watch over the children and assist their study of the Torah. It helps them get their minds off the terrible things that have happened to their families. Please let me know if you have any questions."

"Thank you," Annie said and nodded. The rabbi limped back to his house project.

"It's important that when you hear the spotter yell 'police,' you gather the children and run up the side of the mountain behind the school," Toby said. "You're in more danger than them if you're caught. The *gendarmes* will come."

42

Appeal to self-interest.

Lourdes, France

"I'm going to Marseille," Letty said as she buttoned her dress. "I'm having a French passport made."

"Why?" mother said.

"I need the money you've been saving in the clock." She applied lipstick and eyeliner, and then put her hair up. She didn't have time to argue or let mother deride her.

"Tell me why."

"I met someone that said Switzerland is the best option. I trust them."

"How many times have I told you to drop that stupid idea?" Mother's disparagement no longer had the same effect now that Nicholas confirmed everything she had been hearing.

"Even if we decide not to leave, mother, having fake papers will make us safer."

"Who's making you a passport? How do you know they won't steal our money?"

"I have a contact. I'll wait until they finish the passport."

"I'm not going to Marseille. So how do you expect me to trust this contact of yours?"

"You need the French passport."

"It sounds to me like an excuse for you to go on an adventure."

"Just let me go to make sure it's legitimate." Mother sat for a minute rubbing her hands together. She stared at Letty's red lipstick, but her mind was elsewhere.

"I'll give you the money on one condition."

"Okay."

"Take Suzy with you."

"What if she refuses?"

"What did I say?" It was Blima's way to get her eldest daughter back.

"Okay. Suzy will come."

Letty tracked down Suzy at the hotel, Beauséjour, and knocked on the door. She stared down at her worn dress hanging off her shoulders. There wasn't much to eat over the weeks and months and Letty knew the Richfelds had something to nibble on. Suzy wasn't going to be happy seeing her sister enter her other life, and that made Letty crack a smile.

"Can I help you?" Mrs. Richfeld said, holding the door ajar.

"Is Suzy here?" Letty asked. "I'm her sister, Letty."

"She is. Do come in. Suzy! Your sister is here."

Mr. and Mrs. Richfeld sat close together on a bed, observing. Letty sipped warm water steeped in tea leaves with sugar. It tasted good.

"I'm going to Marseille for a French passport," Letty said.

"Why?" Suzy asked.

"Switzerland. Mother wanted me to get you a passport too."

She was silent looking at Letty not knowing whether to be angry about her invasion of her space. But her youngest sister also extended an opportunity. Suzy looked at the faces in the room and weighed her options.

"What do you think?" Mr. Richfeld said to Suzy.

"When do you leave?" Suzy asked, inspecting Letty's shoes and dress.

"In a few days." Suzy looked at her surrogate parents. Mr. Richfeld wore a buttoned up sweater and Mrs. Richfeld a nice dress. There was a tray of cookies on the table. Letty reached over and took one. Then two. Suzy's focus turned to her sister.

"I don't know, Letty. Do you have a plan?"

Letty nodded.

"Why Switzerland?" she said. The rumor of Switzerland carried with it warnings about being turned over to the Nazis or being shot during the crossing.

"You've heard Switzerland has asylum?" Letty asked.

"I have."

"Suzy," Mr. Richfeld said. "We'll be okay if you go. We're old enough they'll leave us be. It's not safe in France for you. You can get a good smuggler." When Mr. Richfeld spoke, Letty knew Suzy got what she wanted; their permission to leave.

"I'll be sad to leave you, mother," she said to Mrs. Richfeld. "And you too, father." A tear slid down her cheek. Letty's stomach bent inwards at her words and she wanted to retch. It was a perfect tear and it streamed down her left cheek until she caught it with a tissue.

43

There are technicalities, and then there are tricks.

Marseille, France

"Police!" one of the children yelled.

Annie grabbed the hands of two girls and started running up the hill.

"Let's go!" Annie yelled. "Children! Up the hill!" They ran through the long, soggy grass towards the manor house. Annie followed behind up the trail to an outcropping of rocks about fifty yards away above the manor.

She leaned against a rock catching her breath and hiding with the other children behind the boulders.

"Make sure you are behind the rocks," she said. "Don't let anyone see you."

She started counting the kids. Her shoes and ankles were wet and cold from the tall grass.

"We're missing David," Annie said.

"It's a false alarm again!" Toby said hiking up the hill to the rocks. She glared at the kids. "We've told you that this is not a joke. Have you ever heard about the boy who cried wolf?" She caught her breath and stared at each child in the eyes to make a point of her seriousness. "I'm going to find David! No more false alarms!"

In the evening Annie helped the children get ready for bed. She brushed the girls' hair and made sure they climbed into their beds. Before she turned out the lights, she read them Jewish stories. She thought of how excited father got as he told her the stories of Moses and Solomon, and how his eyes got big and his hands flew about when he told her, "Don't go crying Ani Shlomo! No one wants to hear your complaints."

Annie read the story of Miriam from *The Book of Exodus*. "Miriam hid Moses by the side of the river protecting her brother from the Pharaoh, who liked to kill newborn Hebrew boys," Annie read.

"Was Miriam ever married?" a girl said from under the covers, interrupting the story.

"Yes, she was married to Caleb," Annie said.

"Are you married?" Rachel asked.

"I'm not."

"Why not?" Rachel asked. "Is it because of the war?"

Annie nodded.

"My mom's gone because of the war," Rachel said. "I miss her."

Annie sat on the bed with Rachel looking at her soft cheeks. "You will see her again."

She turned off the lamp by the bed. When Annie was done making her rounds shutting off lights she found her bed and crawled under the cold covers and rubbed her feet together for warmth. She wondered where father was and if he was safe. She closed her eyes and drifted to sleep.

When her eyes opened again she heard a car driving up the tree-lined road as headlights lit up the room and the crunch of gravel under its wheels. No one ever came at this time. She threw her covers off and ran to the window. It was two police cars pulling up out front.

Annie didn't know what to do, but on impulse ran down stairs to a side room next to the entrance and near a back door where she hid in the dark and listened. There was pounding at the door and Annie heard the rabbi limp somewhere in the house.

"What's the meaning of this?" the rabbi said. The police visit didn't intimidate him and his Russian accent cut through the sleeping house.

"We have authorization to remove these children," a policeman said. Annie heard the crinkling of paper.

"I need to see these documents you speak of," the rabbi said. There was ruffling of papers. "What's this?"

"They're documents parents signed releasing the children into our custody," a soft-spoken policeman said. "We will reunite them." Annie sat in her nightgown holding her knees in a corner of the dark room behind some chairs. She listened to the voices as they filtered through the hallways of the house.

"Reunite them?" the rabbi said. "Is that some sort of joke?"

"The parents have requested to have their children with them," a policeman said.

"In the camps?"

"It's in the documents."

"I have my own documents showing the parents want their children here," the rabbi said.

"You will deny the will of the parent?" said the soft-spoken policeman. "Surely you can check their signatures to verify the authenticity as well as the dates against your own. We would hate to forcibly remove them, but we will."

Annie heard the rabbi limp to his office. It was an eternity as the rabbi looked through his files and took his time. The policemen said little as they waited, but whispered now and then. Annie tried to hear what they said but it was too low. She didn't dare get up fearing any creak might alert them to her presence. She could be arrested if they checked her papers and she would be taken too.

After a half-hour the rabbi's feet slid along the floor. Even before the rabbi spoke, Annie knew by the slowness of his limp that the rabbi was defeated.

"I am puzzled by the hour you chose to come," the rabbi said. "Come back tomorrow to collect the children."

"We have orders to take them now. Their parents are waiting."

"Whose orders?"

"It's on the documents."

"I see."

"Did the signatures match?" By the tone of his question the policeman was getting impatient.

"I'm hesitant to release these children into your care. The parents explicitly placed these children in my care."

"What will become of them?" the rabbi's wife asked.

"They will be reunited with their parents," the soft-spoken policeman said. "Did the signatures match?"

"They did," the rabbi said.

"There's no problem then," the policeman said. "We will take the children. Do we need to go room to room looking for them? I would hate to wake everyone."

"You stay here. I'll get the children myself."

The rabbi and his wife climbed the stairs to the children's rooms. Annie stayed huddled in a ball listening to the creaking floors above her. She imagined the tired eyes and confusion at the late hour. Children's voices came down the stairs and then the pitter-patter of their feet.

"Where are we going?" one child asked. Annie tried to hear who they were. From the shuffle of feet and voices it sounded like four or five kids.

"To be with your parents, child," the rabbi said.

"Really?" said the boy. There was happiness in his voice.

"These are all the children?" the policeman said. "Pin their names on their shirts." The heels of his boots stomped on the wood floors as a policeman checked each child's name.

Annie heard light footsteps upstairs as the commotion woke the entire house. Children ran to the windows looking out into the darkness, which was illuminated by the police cars' headlight beams. They watched their friends filed out in a single line and put in the cars. Doors clicked open, and then slammed shut. After a few revs of the engine the wheels pushed through the gravel and into the night. Little feet ran from room to room above searching for who was taken.

"Rachel's gone!" Annie heard a child yell to the others.

"So is David!" Another yelled.

"And Leila is gone too!"

Annie closed her eyes feeling the emptiness in the house. In all, six children were taken in the early hours of morning. When Annie crawled out from behind the chairs and went to the front door the rabbi stood in the entrance watching the night. He heard Annie and looked back at her. The smell of exhaust was still in the air.

"It's no longer safe for you here," Rabbi Schneerson said. "They're looking for any reason to arrest us. If they catch you, you will go to an internment camp. It's best if you start making other arrangements."

Why the Vichy wanted the children, Annie didn't find out, but it was likely part of the deal Laval cut with the Germans. She did learn the police promised the parents safety for their families if they revealed where their children hid. In the following days the rabbi began his fight for their release.

44

The tables will turn when you have something of value.

Lourdes, France

Mother popped the back of the clock off, unhitching the latch she rigged to keep the money inside from falling everywhere. She dug her fingers in and pulled the bills out, counting it into piles on their bed.

There was just over 4,000 francs. Letty didn't know how she fit it in there and she wasn't sure it was enough to cover the fake papers. She hoped Suzy had money too.

"I'll get you a passport," Letty said. Blima found a picture she had taken a year ago for her Polish documents. She slid the little head shot into the paperwork. Mother handed her the clock.

"What do I need this for?" Letty said.

"It still works," she said. "Put it in your things." Letty shimmied by the bed they shared and around a chair blocking the door. Mother grabbed a headscarf off the Cross that hung on the wall and tied it over her hair before they left for the station.

The Richfelds and Suzy waited at the edge of the station platform. Mother's hands were clasped together. She looked over at Suzy standing. When the train pulled up Suzy went to her and gave mother a quick hug before returning to the old couple. Mrs. Richfeld ran her hands over Suzy's hair and rubbed out a wrinkle on her dress. Mother watched them hug as if it were another family. The train whistle blew and the smoke and steam filled the station and the two sisters boarded.

"It's a lucky day having pretty girls in my train car," the conductor said as he took Suzy's ticket. He came back and gave her candy, which she tossed in her bag.

Letty and Suzy didn't say much to each other. Suzy sat in the aisle seat and enticed the conductor to come by and talk. Maybe she saw him as protection in case police searched for Jews and asked for documents. She reached into her bag and pulled out the candies, handing Letty one, and started sucking on another. When the conductor came by she gave him one too. He smiled and thanked her. Letty knew she always had ulterior motives.

When he walked back down the train car she spit the candy out into her hand.

"What's the plan, Letty?" she asked.

"Get Annie and then the documents," she said in a whisper.

"Have you thought this out?"

"I know what I'm doing."

"Where are we staying?"

"At the school with Annie." But Letty didn't know where they were staying. She didn't know if Annie was still at the school, but assumed if they hadn't heard from her, she was there. Aside from the address of the forger, and a name on a map of where to cross, Letty didn't know what she was doing.

"Do we have enough money?"

"I hope so," Letty said. "Do you have any?"

She nodded, but the question ended the conversation and Suzy returned to gazing around the car. It had been a couple years since they spent this much time with each other. Suzy carried herself with an air of superiority that intimidated others. Passengers glanced at her, unable to resist a quick stare, and then diverted their eyes when her head turned their direction.

Letty never knew Suzy very well as a child, only that she ruled over her, and that she was mother's favorite. But now the world was different and Letty offered her something of value. It was a weird new dynamic even as Suzy tried to project her authority over her. Letty saw Suzy's insecurity more clearly the harder she tried to control her surroundings. Suzy was here only because Letty needed mother to give her the money. She didn't intimidate her as she once did; instead Letty shut her eyes. "Letty." Suzy tried to talk but she didn't answer. Soon Letty was rocked to sleep by the train car.

45

Save one life, and you will save an entire world.

Marseille, France

The throngs of people pushed at Letty to get out of the way as she stepped off the train in Marseille. Suzy dangled from the railcar door searching for an exit above the crowd.

"This way," she said grabbing Letty's hand. People parted for her and in a minute they were outside and on the street.

Behind them *gendarmes* asked two men to show their identification cards. "I also have some really good chocolate from Brussels," Suzy said. "I want to make them last, but I might let you try some." Letty looked over her shoulder.

They climbed aboard the bus towards the outskirts and it lurched through the gridlocked streets. Soon the avenues of spewing smoke and traffic jams turned into the surrounding mountains studded with jagged boulders and chaparral, and Letty tugged Suzy's arm and they got off the bus.

"I think this it," Letty said. "The big house on the hill." They walked up the tree-lined street and there were dots of people moving around in grassy meadows on the hillside by the house. When they came to the front of the large manor a man limped towards them with a big red beard.

"Hello," he said pulling his hands out of his jacket pockets. "How can I help you?"

"We're Annie's sisters. I'm Suzy and this is Letty. Is she here?"

"I don't know if she's left yet." He looked over at a girl sitting on a chair. "Sara, is Annie here?"

"Where did she go?" Suzy asked.

"She was going to the city. Things have been difficult."

"She's still here," Sara said. "Toby has left."

Annie came out of the house and Suzy ran up and wrapped her arms around her sister.

"I'm happy you're still here!" Suzy said. "We came to see you."

Annie didn't know what to say. She was shocked at seeing her sisters. "I was leaving. The *gendarmes* are raiding all over the city, even here."

They sat on the side of the house to eat something. In the evening light looking into the valley little plumes of smoke wafted into the air from chimneys as farmers prepared their suppers. Children ran through the house, tugging at each other's shirts and pulling at arms. One child came up to Letty and tapped her on the shoulder.

"Are you living with us now?" he asked.

"I don't think so," Letty said.

After they ate Rabbi Schneerson leaned against the side of the house and stared into the distance. He stroked his beard.

"From the Talmud we know whoever destroys a soul, is considered to have destroyed an entire world," he said, his Russian accent thick, but his words crisp as his eyes locked with Letty's. "But, whoever saves a life, one life, is considered to have saved an entire world. And saving all the worlds that are created from that one life. Even as I say this I know the police will come again and again. You must leave; I know I cannot protect you here."

"What about Switzerland?" Letty asked the rabbi.

"I've heard people smuggled their children into Switzerland," the rabbi said. "The French and Swiss are patrolling the border. People that get caught by either side are sent to French concentration camps. And some are turned over to the Germans. Do you have enough money for the trip? Smugglers are expensive."

"We have some," Letty said. "Not much. A little over 4,000 francs."

"That won't be enough."

"How much are smugglers?"

"I don't know for sure. Expensive. 5,000 francs a person? Maybe? Also, consider their trustworthiness when choosing one. Smugglers have left refugees on the border to be arrested. Even guided them over the border, shot them, and taken their money."

The girls were silent and Letty didn't want them to get cold feet from the rabbi's words so she changed the subject.

"5,000?" Letty said. "Sheesh."

"The Children's Aid Society in Marseille might be able to help. Tell them I sent you."

There was nowhere else for them to go, except the Lerners in Marseille. After the raids, only Mr. and Mrs. Lerner were safe because of their old age. Toby and Leah stayed outside the city hiding with their brothers through Josiah's contacts.

When they arrived at the rooming house in the heart of Marseille, which was already cramped with two small beds, Mr. Lerner grumbled. He didn't have to say a thing; his stare was enough to say he didn't approve. They took up space in his small room, but he also didn't like their clothing choices, make-up and uncovered hair. Mr. Lerner's Orthodox ways didn't budge. He wore his long beard and preached the virtues of religion. Mrs. Lerner always wore a scarf and a warm smile.

In the morning they searched for Letty's contact for fake passports. There was an address, and the name, "Francois." It was a warm day in late September and the southern French city radiated with heat.

They walked through the narrow streets by a public swimming pool, a grocery store, blocks of apartments and found the building. It was an optometrist shop. Letty walked in as Annie and Suzy waited outside. A woman sat at a desk with a little screwdriver tightening the side of spectacles. Her hair hung over her face.

"I'll be right with you," she said without looking up. "Are you here to pick up your glasses?" she asked.

"No," Letty said.

"You need glasses?"

"Well, no."

"How can I help you?"

"I'm looking for Francois."

"There's no Francois here."

"Are you sure?"

"Do you see any Francois here? It's just me right now. I'm in the middle of something. If you don't mind." She returned to the frames that sat under a lamp.

"I must've been mistaken," Letty said. "My friend, Nicholas, said Francois was here." The woman looked at Letty and then outside through the barred windows of the shop at her sisters. She was a little older than Suzy, with dark hair.

"Many people come for Francois. Some might be police, but I know the name, Nicholas. Try next door." She nodded her head to the right.

The door was peeling around a peephole and a rusting deadbolt sealed the door shut. Letty knocked and they waited outside for several minutes. She knocked again. There were footsteps and a person stopped on the other side. Then the bolt flipped and the door opened. An older man poked his head out. He had a large forehead, wore glasses, and had a thin well shaven face. "Yes?" he said.

"Nicholas said to come see you," she said.

"Come in," he said looking down the street both ways. On the other side of the door were stairs and they climbed up into the dark room. "Sorry for the wait. I was in the middle of some work. Please have a seat." His voice was both professional and kind. There were chairs set up like a doctor's waiting room and he had his desk in the corner. A camera on a tripod with a large flashbulb was set up next to a table with a paper cutter.

189

"How can I help you?"

"We need French passports," Suzy said.

"By when?" He folded his hands together on the desk. Suzy looked at Letty.

"As soon as possible," she said.

"I can have them in two days," he said. "The cost is 3000 francs per passport and that includes the photo. I'll need half upfront." Letty added it up in her head. They didn't have enough.

"So for four passports that's 12,000 francs?" she asked. His eyes scanned their faces.

"Well, I count only three of you. That is 9,000. 4,500 upfront."

"Yes, but we need one for my mother as well," Letty said.

"Where is she?" he asked.

"She's in Lourdes," she said. "But I have a picture."

"Let me see the photo," he said flipping his hand and showing impatience. Letty pulled it out and handed it over. He looked at it and his brows furrowed making his large forehead even larger.

"This is why I require my customers to come in person," he said. "This photo will never work. You see how her body is parallel to the camera. It's more a beauty shot, than a passport photo. It's subtle, but a dead-give-away for a forgery. I cannot make one with this. I'm sorry. It'll be spotted in an instant."

"This is all we have," Letty said. "Can you please try? We'll pay you." He shook his head, no. He pulled out a passport and opened the first page.

"See the difference between the two photos?" There was a slight difference, but she also saw it was impossible to plead with him and his fastidious attention to detail, or maybe he was overwhelmed by the shear amount of people asking for passports. There were stacks of passports behind him.

"You see all these passports? I'm working on all of them right now."

"Okay," she said.

Letty dug into her bag and pulled out the money. She counted out

4,000 francs onto his desk. She only had 100 francs left. They needed more.

"Can I give you 4,000 upfront?" Letty said.

"I need 4,500." There was no budging in his eyes.

"Annie, do you have any?" she said.

"I have 150," she said.

"Suzy, I need 350," Letty said. Letty guessed Suzy had thousands the Richfelds gave her. But she didn't let on.

"Can you take 4,150?" Suzy said to Francois leaning forward in her chair. "We have the rest of the money back where we're staying."

He shook his head. Suzy sat back in her chair and stared at a mirror etched with three deer huddled in the background and pulled out a stack of cash. She counted out 350 francs, and put the rest in her bag.

"Let's proceed," Francois said. He tapped the bills together and placed the money in a metal box.

They each stood in front of a blank canvas and Francois instructed them to face forward and stare directly into the camera lens. He held out the flash and there was a blinding light that popped.

"Try not to blink," he said. "Keep your eyes wide and suck in your cheeks a little. Keep a straight face." Francois went to his desk and took out a notebook. "I'm going to create a profile for each of you. What name do you want for your passport?"

"How about, Piccard," Letty said.

"That was the first lady of France," Francois said. "Marie Louise Picard."

"It was?" she said. "I thought it was the last name of a scientist who made hot-air balloons? Auguste Piccard."

"Well, whatever it was, it'll work fine," he said. "You're now, Marie Louise Picard. You were named after the first lady. Your birthplace will be, Lille, France, which is on the border of Belgium. That will explain your accent. You will be a student." Letty kept her actual birthdate so it was easily remembered.

After Suzy and Annie took their pictures, chose their names (Rene

191

Picard for Suzy, and Antoinette Picard for Annie) Francois showed them out, looking through the peephole before opening the door.

"Your passports will be done in two days," he said. That was two days to find the rest of the money, and a passport for mother.

46

Sometimes you need to ask for more.

"How much money do you have Suzy?" Letty asked.

"Not enough," she said.

"What do you mean?"

"I'm saving it to put towards a smuggler. For us!"

"The Children's Aid Society," Annie said, breaking in before her sisters screamed at each other on the street. "Rabbi Schneersohn mentioned them. When the rabbi tried to get the children back after the raid he went to the Hotel Bompard. It's a refugee camp for Jewish children downtown. They run a school there."

The sea air blew through the bus windows, soothing the skin from the burning sun. The bus came to a stop. "Hotel Bompard," the driver said and pointed. They heard children playing on the other side of the hotel's wall, but no one was in sight.

They waited across the street under the shade of a tree nervous about detection from patrolling *gendarmes*. Hotel Bompard was a Jewish refugee transit camp. Women and children were held inside waiting to be moved to the larger internment camps of Gurs and Drancy. Bousquet had arrested thousands in Paris, and followed that with another dragnet of more than 7,000 Jews in the Southern Zone of France, which included Marseille.[1]

Letty looked for someone with an "honest face" to approach. The front door of the hotel opened and an older man in a white collared shirt, slacks and a stethoscope emerged. He was about to get into his car when she jumped up.

"*Excusez-moi*," she said. The man looked at her surprised. He placed his black leather bag into his car. "We have travelled from Lourdes—"

"If your children are inside, I can't help you," he said pointing to the hotel.

"No, but we're looking for the Children Aid Society. Do you know where they are?" He stared at her.

"Yes," he said.

"Are they inside? Can we can talk to someone?"

He thought for a moment.

"Their offices are on Rue d'Italie, downtown." He got into his car and turned the engine on. "I have to get to my next stop, but I'm going that way and can give you a ride."

They climbed in and his wheels screeched as he drove by the walled neighborhoods covered in bougainvillea bushes with red flowers and thorns climbing up liked beautiful, barbed wire.

"You work at Hotel Bompard?" Annie asked.

"Yes," he said. "I examine all the refugees in camps around Marseille."

"Are there a lot?" Annie said.

"Around nine thousand interned." He parked on the street and pointed to the building. "The offices you are looking for are inside there."

There were a couple of women typing at desks. No one took notice of the three young women that stood in front of them in the office. They were too busy.

"Hello," Letty said. A woman lifted her head. "We are looking for assistance."

"Philippe, visitors," the woman said, and continued typing. A man emerged from an office, disheveled, but tucking his shirt in an attempt to be presentable.

"Bousquet found a way to revoke the exit visas for the children," he said to the other lady and set a stack of papers on her desk. "It seems the U.S. embassy is also backing off its pressure. Write a letter to the Italian embassy." He turned his attention to Letty and her sisters. "I'm Philippe. How can we help you?"

"We want to leave France," Letty said.

"Do you have a guide?" he said.

"Guide? A smuggler? We have a plan and documents in order. We just need assistance for the trip."

"You're looking for money?" he asked.

"We want a guide too," Suzy said. "Money is needed to finish paying for our documents, and for a smuggler."

He scanned their faces, but his mind was on other issues. The women were typing in the background, so focused they didn't even raise their eyes once in Letty's direction.

"We were staying at Rabbi Schneersohn outside Marseille," Annie said. "He said it's no longer safe there. He said you could help."

"Can I see your I.D.," he said looking at Annie. They pulled them out of the bags mother had made. "You have paperwork for the trip? Which country?"

"Switzerland," Letty said. "We don't have enough money though." He walked to a safe and opened it, pulling out a stack of French Francs and a ledger.

"I'm going to give you 10,000 francs for the three of you," he said writing into the thick black book and adding it to the legions of other names. He handed Letty the money. "Good luck." He turned around and started talking with one of the women typing. It was a lot of money, but it wasn't going to cover a smuggler after they finished paying for the passports.

They caught a bus back to the Lerners' rooming house and Letty's thoughts were on how to get mother a French passport. She knew mother was against going to Switzerland and would never agree if she didn't have the papers.

"We need to find a smuggler," Suzy said. "It's the only way mother will make the trip."

"There's not enough," Letty said.

"Why didn't you ask for more? You just took what he gave you."

"Why didn't you?"

"I would've if I'd known you were going walk away like that. He didn't know our money situation. We barely have enough for our passports."

Mr. Lerner was in the middle of *maariv*, the evening prayer when they walked into the room. He closed the Torah looking down and sighing at the interruption. He stroked his long, scraggly beard and looked at them with dark eyes.

"Where have you been?" he said to Annie in Hebrew.

"We're making arrangements to leave for Switzerland," Annie said.

"Oh, I see," he said. "Are you hiring a smuggler?"

"We don't have money for that," Annie said. "We're getting papers, but we still need one for mother. Our contact won't make her one."

"There's a man in Lyon," he said. "He'll make her a passport." Mr. Lerner picked up a pencil and scribbled the name and where to find him on a paper and handed it to her.

"Thank you!" Annie said. It was an unexpected contact that gave them hope.

Mrs. Lerner lay under the covers ready for sleep. Mr. Lerner opened the Torah again and his lips moved over the *Shema*, the last words said for the day. He closed the Torah and hobbled into bed next to his wife.

[1] Maurice Rajsfus, *La Police de Vichy. Les Forces de l'ordre françaises au service de la Gestapo, 1940/1944*, Le Cherche-midi éditeur, 1995. Chapter XIV, *La Bataille de Marseille*, pp. 209–217.

47

Watch out for those hiding behind a cloak of piety.

Letty tried on the cheapest swimsuits in a store near the pool. In the changing room the tight rayon felt uncomfortable. This was her first suit. It seemed weird wearing underwear in public, but now they at least blended in with the French women going to the pool.

Letty gave the cashier 120 francs, the equivalent of about two dollars. The pool was down the street from where they were to pick up the passports. The large wall encircling the pool had vines of ivy creeping up and over the sides. The water had a greenish tint and there were no lifeguards, but plenty of French men and women lying around the side of it, dangling their legs into its coolness. It was approaching fall, but a heat spell was cooking the city.

Letty tilted her face back to the sun and the rays beat into her skin. The war didn't seem to exist at the pool with its strange carnal attractions: arms, calves, chests and much more. Annie kept her dress on and sat next to Letty, while Suzy strode around the pool attracting glances from the French men. She knew how to walk in her swimsuit with a well-practiced stride. It worked with one bold Frenchman jumping up to help her down the ladder into the pool. She gave a casual giggle and pushed herself into the water.

Letty waited for a moment when one man pushed another into

the pool causing a huge splash, and a distraction to slip into the water. She dropped in, not gracefully, but well-enough not to attract stares. Paddling less like a dog this time, she bumped through the other bobbing bodies, working her way to the shallow end. Annie sat watching from the edge, a better swimmer than her, but too shy to join. Suzy was splashing with another Frenchman. He lifted her up. Watching the churn and ripples from the hedonistic commotion Letty thought about Theo. He would have commented on the insanity of sitting around a cement body of water while the mountains were so close and a war was going on, but she enjoyed the small fact that Bousquet's *gendarmes* were searching for them, and they sat by the pool! How *Candide*!

By late afternoon her skin was getting pink and she needed to pull Suzy from her new group of friends across the water. They put their dresses back on and left the concrete pool, drunk from the sun, faces glowing, and hair damp. As they stepped from the pool's door, there was a group of *gendarmes* in their high boots and cylinder hats patrolling across the street. The sisters put their heads down, trying to avoid the *gendarmes'* attention.

"Hey, you, Ladies!" a *gendarme* yelled, his hands clutching his belt. "Stop!"

They looked at each other, so close to having their fake papers and now being stopped, the irony was hard to miss. Their paperwork from Lourdes showed that they were Jews from Belgium. Bousquet was looking for foreign Jews just like them and his police were pulling people on the streets with spot checks like this one.

They stopped and faced the four policemen walking toward them. Letty tried to read their faces for any signal as they got nearer and crossed the street, making a car stop for them. The man that yelled at them clomped up to Suzy.

"Hello Madame," he said. "It's a fine afternoon. Did you enjoy the pool?"

"It was nice," Suzy said. Her face had a forced, wry smile.

"We've been roasting in the sun all day—" he said.

"You must be hot in that uniform," Suzy said. "You would've enjoyed the pool."

"It's really hot," he said. "Why are you ladies in such a hurry? Do we make you nervous?" He was fishing for something. The police towered above them. They weren't tall girls, but these men were huge.

"What do you mean?" Suzy looked at Letty, and then at the police.

"What I mean is that we'll be off in an hour. How about you ladies join us for a drink? We can get out of these hot uniforms." The *gendarmes* all started laughing. She giggled.

"I don't know if we can—" Letty said. The police stared at her for a second and returned their gaze to Suzy.

"When is good for you?" Suzy said to the *gendarme*. She ignored Letty.

"Now is good," he said. His cheeks got flush and rocked backed on his heels. The other *gendarmes* stood around them all holding their belts and their grins were almost as shiny as the knee-high boots they wore. Annie was next to Letty, saying nothing, but forcing a smile. Suzy was like a maestro and giggled more. Her cheeks looked red too, but probably from the heat of the sun.

"That sounds great," she said. "Let's go!"

"Okay," he said.

"Frederic," said the *gendarme* with blond hair coming out from his hat. "We need to file our reports first."

"Nonsense," he said. "We can escort these fine ladies." He was taller than the others, bigger, and commanded them to his will.

"Where shall we go?" Suzy said.

"There's a nice restaurant down the street where one can get a glass of wine."

"Well let's go." Suzy grabbed her sisters' arms, pulling them in that direction.

"We are on duty," another officer said.

"You're right," Frederic said to the officer. "Ladies, since we are on duty I'm going to ask you for identification. It's part of my duty."

Letty's heart jumped. Suzy reached into her bag and started fishing for I.D. without pause. The officers watched her pulling her stuff out. "Candies?" She offered them her favorite caramels.

"That's okay," he said. "Don't worry about your I.D. I'll check it later." He gave her a grin. "Little Pepe is right. We have to finish our work. It won't take long." Annie shifted her bag onto her shoulder and let out a sigh.

"Ahhh, okay," Suzy said. "That'll give us a chance to freshen up for you."

"Give us an hour," he said. "Meet us at that café over there." He pointed down the street.

"We'll see you there," she said and smiled at him. "Don't work too hard." With that she clasped her sisters' arms pulling them up the street with speed, but not too fast and slowed her sisters.

"Hey!" he yelled after them. Letty's heart skipped. They turned.

"One hour!" he said.

"One hour!" Suzy said, waving.

"We're not going back there," Annie said.

"Of course not," Suzy said, "but he sure is going to be mad!" They all started laughing and couldn't stop. Their laughs echoed off the building walls and Letty looked over her shoulder to make sure they didn't hear.

By the time they made it back to the Lerner's room it was late. Unlike before, Mrs. Lerner was in one bed, and Mr. Lerner was in the other. They breathed deep and Mrs. Lerner was snoring, not loud, but with a gurgle that made you worry she wasn't getting enough air.

"Who's sleeping where?" Letty said in a whisper.

"I'm on the floor," Annie said. Without saying anything Suzy slid into the bed with the snoring woman. That left only the bed with the old, bearded man. Mr. Lerner rolled over making a little room for Letty. She left her dress on and climbed in.

She lay on the edge of the bed. Any closer and she'd fall on Annie.

The sun drained her and she closed her eyes forgetting about Mr. Lerner sleeping beside her. The soft swallows of air from Mrs. Lerner reverberated in her ears and she drifted into a deep sleep. Her dreams were vivid. She saw the sharpness of greys, whites and blacks of the pool. A boy was swimming upside down his feet poking out of the water with Suzy standing on them pointing as she rode through the water. A hand pulled her shoulder as she sat on the concrete. "Your passport!" the big *gendarme* said. "I need to see your passport!"

"Tomorrow, I can give it to you tomorrow!"

"Now!" he said. Letty tried to speak, but her mouth was sewn closed. "Answer me!"

"See what you caused, Letty!" mother said to her. She held a needle and thread. "This is your fault. Your foolishness. If you didn't go to the pool you wouldn't have caused this mess!"

A *gendarme* grabbed her arm and pulled her through the pool into a wall of ivy.

"Passport!" the *gendarme* said. His face grew like a balloon and was about to pop. He grabbed her arm and then her shoulder and pinned her down on the concrete. She looked at the naked bodies dangling their feet in the pool. They watched yet did nothing. She tried to yell, "help." Nothing came out. He rubbed his hands over her legs, his barrel body crushing her and she couldn't breathe.

Letty's eyes popped open from her dream and her body was still pinned and Mr. Lerner's scraggly beard rubbed against her face. What is going on? His hands rubbed over her chest like old pieces of sand paper, snagging the fibers of her dress sending shivers through her body. This pious old man moved his hand under the covers pulling at her dress and forcing his hand on her thigh before she realized it was no accident. She grabbed his paw as it crept up her leg and pushed him off. He struggled and kissed at her neck, and when his beard tickled her, she gagged. Mrs. Lerner snored not four feet away in a bed shared with Suzy, and Annie breathed in deep sleep below Letty on the ground.

She gave him a strong elbow. "Get off," she said under her breath, as she didn't want to cause a scene. Only then did this "religious" man roll over and go to sleep. She felt embarrassed for him. He soon was breathing deep, and Letty lay there with her eyes wide open staring at the varying shades of greys and blacks of the dark room. She didn't dare close her eyes, or move, stuck in this bed with a man who just groped her.

As soon as there was a glow of light coming through the window Mr. Lerner got up at the end of the bed and stepped over Annie. He wrapped his *tefillin*, small leather boxes holding scrolls, around his forehead and then all the way up his left arm with a methodic intensity from years of practice. He opened his Torah and recited the *Pesukei desimra*, his praises for God.

Letty said nothing and lay there listening to the hollowness of the words he read in Hebrew. Big, sloshing words, rolled off his tongue in a harsh tone and rhythm that was only theater. She remembered when mother told her she wasn't allowed to say "God" in the bathroom. She smirked at how scared she was the first time she said, "God," and how she waited for the lightning bolt to strike her down. It didn't matter what this man read, his actions weren't protected by the prayers. His Orthodox adherence didn't make him any better than anyone else. He was living a lie. She knew it and he couldn't escape that.

She didn't dare get up until Dora Lerner and her sisters rose. Mr. Lerner sat reading as they got ready to leave and didn't look up.

"Thank you for letting us stay," Annie said to Mrs. Lerner. "Thank you Mr. Lerner for the contact in Lyon. We're going to get papers for mother."

He looked up for a brief moment to acknowledge Annie and put his head back in the book without even a nod. It wasn't dismissive, more like he had more important things in his book that these girls were keeping him from. Letty hoped he was looking for penance in the depths of its pages, but doubted it entered his mind. Instead she saw him hiding in its flaps and folds, picking and choosing the convenient, righteous commandment, to sooth his dirty secrets.

48

Finish what you start.

"We could save our money and put it towards a smuggler," Suzy said. They were walking toward Francois's apartment.

"What do you mean?" Letty said. "We've already put down 4,500."

"If we find a good smuggler, we won't need passports." Suzy had a point.

"Do you know a smuggler we can trust? That will take four people for 10,000 francs? You've heard the rumors about smugglers leaving people stranded on the border, even killing them."

"We're making a mistake not saving the money for a smuggler," Suzy said.

"Do you have enough money for a smuggler?" Suzy didn't answer. "Do you?"

Letty knocked on the door and heard a commotion of activity inside. Voices and footsteps murmured through the door. It opened and a different man stood facing them.

"Yes?" he said.

"We're here for a pick up," Letty said. "Francois, is he here?" He waved them in.

The room was filled with a large family, and several other people, all wanting forged papers. The camera's flash popped. The family of four children, father and mother, and grandparents sat quiet while Francois took information from another couple. Some forgers made up to 30 passports an hour and Francois had a backlog with stacks of files on his desk. With Bousquet working with the Nazis in Southern France planning *razzias*, Jews were trying to flee in hordes. Not one of them knew where to go for sure, only rumors, educated guesses and luck. Letty decided it was Switzerland. Others thought it was an awful plan, like mother.

"Okay," he said to the couple. "Your names?" He looked at Letty as he wrote. "I have your passports ready. Just a moment."

When the couple got up he pulled Letty and her sisters' passports from a drawer and handed them to Letty. She looked at the documents. Oh, what a terrible photo. "My face looks fat and round," Letty said. But it had an official stamp and seal and all her information, "Nationalite: Francais." She counted out the 4,500. Letty was now, "Marie Louise Picard."

They had around 5,500 francs left. At least 3,000 of it was for mother's passport and the rest was for travel. Smugglers cost as much as 5,000 francs a person. It was almost out of the question. By buying the forgeries Letty almost ensured they were going to have to make the journey on their own.

49

When backed into a corner, you will take unnecessary risks.

Lyon, France

The dry mountains of the Mediterranean turned into rolling pastures as their train headed to Lyon. The French city was about two hours from Geneva, Switzerland.

From the station a bus dropped them near the Grande Synagogue, which Mrs. Lerner said sheltered Jewish refugees. There was a large room with straw and all around women and children were sprawled out, some coughing, others looking through their bags. Children played cards and ran through the hall and Letty searched for an empty spot in the straw to put their things. Almost every space was taken.

Annie was quiet, but that wasn't surprising. She often kept to herself blending into the background. When Letty looked at her for the first time since they left Marseille, she was sitting in the hay, her face drained of blood and her lips coated with a thin chalk like substance.

"Are you okay?" Letty asked.

Annie heaved into the hay vomiting out what little food she had in her stomach. Beads of sweat formed on her upper lip and forehead, and straw stuck to her cheeks tangling in her hair. She reached into her sweater pocket searching for something and pulled out a piece of paper.

"The address." Her voice was faint as a whisper and she curled up into a ball. On the crumpled paper was the name of the man that made forged papers, "Isaak." Letty got some water for Annie and wiped her forehead. She scooped up the dirty hay as Suzy blocked the view of snooping refugees.

"I'll find this man," Letty said. She folded the paper, grabbed most of the money and mother's photo and left the synagogue.

Lyon is sandwiched between two rivers, the Rhone and the Saone. The synagogue sat on the Saone River and Letty walked over the Rhone River crossing a bridge to find Rue Salomon Reinach. She came to a square and on the corner at the address was a restaurant. She checked the address to make sure before going in, remembering Francois's forgery shop.

"Will you be dining with us, Madame," a waiter said.

"I'm looking for Isaak."

"Isaak's not here."

"Does he work here?"

"No, no, but he comes in."

"Where can I find him?"

"Don't know. If you leave a contact, I'll give it to him." She wrote the Grande Synagogue down and her name.

"It's important he gets it." She folded the paper and handed it to him.

"Okay, if I see him," he said putting the paper in his pocket.

Letty wasn't sure if it was the right spot as she walked out and double-checked the address outside. The waiter said he knew Isaak, yet it all seemed a tad off. Something wasn't right.

"You're back already?" Suzy said.

"He wasn't there."

Annie's face was greenish and her hair clung to her temples. Letty sat down and felt her forehead. It was burning up. Letty stared at the straw and the spider webs that spread through the cracks in the stone wall.

"We need to get a hotel," Letty said.

They lifted Annie up as the other refugees watched holding their children back worried they'd catch her flu. Letty carried the suitcases as Suzy held Annie's arm for support. They tried to leave through the front, but a woman stopped them.

"Are any of you, Letty?" she asked.

"I'm Letty. My sister is sick. We need to find a place for her to stay."

"A man left you this."

Letty unfolded the paper, "Meet at the fountain at Rue du Plat and Rue Clotilde Bizolon at 6pm. Izaak." He spelled his name different than Letty thought, but it was the forger.

"It's from him," she said. "Is this near by?" She showed the woman the address.

"It's close."

They found a cheap room nearby for Annie. At 5 o'clock Letty left for the fountain to meet Izaak. She watched the cars drive around the circle and the five streets, which converged onto the fountain. Izaak could come from any direction and she didn't know what he looked like.

"Are you Letty?" a short man said in French, but with an Eastern European accent. He was in his forties with short hair and stubble on his face. He came from behind the fountain where Letty sat.

"Izaak?" Letty asked.

"Yes." He sat down next to her as cars whipped by rattling and spewing smoke over the street. She coughed and wiped her eyes.

"I was given your name. I need papers for my mother."

"I can do that."

"Are they good quality?"

"Of course. I use one. I'm Jewish refugee. From Poland." He took out a French passport and showed her. His name in the passport was "Izaak." The quality looked good, like the ones they just got from Francois. If mother got one of that quality it would be hard for her not

207

to come.

"My mother is from Poland," Letty said.

"You have photo?" Letty handed it to him and he examined it. "Yes, this can be used."

"Another forger said it wasn't good enough. French officials would see it was a fake."

"I crop it. Will work fine."

"You sure?"

"Yes, yes."

"Okay, how much?"

"3,000."

"3,000?" She looked at his hands and then his eyes for any clue to his character. The fountain sprayed little streams of water out of cherubs' vases and the splashes hit their backs. He didn't face Letty and instead watched the cars zip around the circle.

"3,000 upfront," he said.

"1,500 now. 1,500 when I get it."

"No. You want passport. 3,000 now."

"Fine. It's okay to give it to you here?" This wasn't someone she met on the street. He was referred.

"Sure. Not a problem."

She pulled the money out of her dress pocket and counted the money right in the circle laying it on the thin edge of the fountain. A passing *gendarme* might have suspected them of a backroom deal, but no *gendarmes* walked by. She handed him the crumpled, dirty bills.

Izaak took the money and he stuffed it into his inside jacket pocket.

"The photo?"

"Oh, here's her photo." She handed him mother's picture.

"I bring papers to synagogue."

"No, we don't stay there now. We are at a hotel. On Rue Victor Hugo—"

"Okay, write it. I bring it there tomorrow." She handed him the address.

"Thank you," she said. He got up and he glanced over his shoulder, not at her, but at one of the streets converging into the circle. He ran across the circle and disappeared up the opposite direction Letty was going. She didn't think to ask what time he was delivering the passport.

As she passed the shops she noticed the berets that French women wore, made popular by the movies and stars like Greta Garbo. She stopped in a shop and browsed the clothes finding berets sitting in a stack. With the wad of money left in her pocket she bought three berets, and saw a map of France, "Carte Michelin De La France," that sat by the cashier. He gave her change and she stuffed the hats and map in her sweater.

Annie was sleeping when she returned to the hotel room. Letty sat back, feeling relief. Mother's lack of French speaking was a liability, but at least the French passport gave her some protection.

50

Keep to the plan and modify as needed.

Annie shivered and they piled every blanket in the room on top of her. Nothing warmed her and she pulled her legs to her chest.

"Can you get me my sweater?" she said. Her forehead was burning up, even as Letty dabbed her face with cool water.

"When's he bringing the papers?" Suzy said.

"He said today, but didn't give a time. It's only 2 o'clock. It took Francois three days to make our papers," Letty said to Suzy, but she was getting more nervous with every passing minute. She rubbed her thumb against her palm. It felt clammy. Where was this guy?

She went to the lobby to check if there were any messages. Nothing. She waited watching the street and every man that walked by. The thought crossed her mind; if Izaak decided to run with their money there was no way to track him down. At four o'clock a pit formed in her stomach. She thought about the road he took from the fountain and if finding him was possible. Of course it was not. Maybe he went to the synagogue. She ran over and asked the woman if a man had come for her. "No." She thought about going to the restaurant to confront the waiter.

At six o'clock she still held hope that he was coming. She paced on the sidewalk outside the hotel and then went back into the lobby. A pit in her belly was turning into the acceptance that he stole their money and wasn't going to show with mother's papers. At 7 o'clock her acceptance turned into anger. This man, a Jewish refugee, stole money from another Jewish refugee. "I hope the Nazis tore this man limb from limb." She wanted him to land in the worst concentration camp.

She bottled her rage and went to the restaurant. "Do you know where I can find Izaak?" Letty asked a man cleaning glasses. He didn't know who he was. The waiter from before wasn't there and she never got his name, so she returned to the hotel.

"Where is he?" Suzy asked.

"I don't think he's coming," she said sitting down and putting her face in her hands. "He stole our money."

"The thief!" Suzy said. "Letty, how did this happen?"

"He just took the money, Suzy! He didn't come back! It was that easy!"

"What do we do about mother?" Suzy said.

"We can convince her to come with us without the papers," Annie said. She was not able to move with the aches in her muscles.

"Who will go?" Letty asked. There was silence amongst the sisters. Annie was sick and Suzy went to her bag and pulled clothes out looking for something.

"I'll go," Letty said. "I need to leave now. It'll take a couple days to get to mother." She felt responsible for losing the money and not getting a passport. It was her plan.

Letty unfolded the map she bought at the shop, and ran her hand over the crinkles and creases. She checked the distance from Lyon to Lourdes, and then Lyon to the Swiss border, and found Annemasse. "It looks like a long trip to Lourdes. It's better if you go to Aix-les-Bains from here. I'll meet you two there with mother. Get a room near the train station and I'll find you." She looked at Suzy and then at Annie to see if they agreed. Their blank faces told her it was settled. "Annie, can you travel?"

"We'll leave tomorrow," Suzy said.

"I forgot I have these." Letty handed each of them a French beret she bought a day earlier. "To help us blend in." Suzy inspected the blue beret, looking at the cloth and the seams and the maker.

"I have one already," she said handing it back. "Give it to mother when you see her. What are you going to say?"

Letty shrugged and shook her head.

51

The person making the recommendation matters.

The night train was so full there was not even standing room. Men and women crammed in shoulder to shoulder. The only space was on the steps outside the car where Letty huddled, wrapped in her scarf, as the ground whipped underneath into darkness. The lights twinkled in the distance as they steamed toward Toulouse with Lourdes lingering far in the distance. Away from her sisters, and without a passport to give mother, her body crumpled in defeat on the edge of the train. She cried into her hands. It was the worst she ever felt knowing she had to deliver the news to mother; they failed to get her the document.

Her anger at the man who stole their money turned to sadness and she no longer saw any difference in the Jews and the Vichy French who rounded them up. She didn't want to be Jewish or to be part of victims victimizing victims.

It was Mr. Lerner who was worse than the man who took their money. He was the creep that recommended him. She should have known! What was she thinking trusting someone Mr. Lerner suggested. She knew that there was only herself to blame for that.

Letty kept replaying it in her mind. Why didn't she recognize the red flags from that man? In retrospect it was easy to spot the con. The public places they met. The waiter at the restaurant was probably in on it and got a cut. Demanding all the money upfront. They were desperate to get mother papers. Why did she give all the money to him? She should have insisted on holding back half. Letty screamed at the night, and then returned her face to her hands to sob alone.

The violent wind tossed her hair around the beret as she hunched over the side of the train stairs. A small bump in the track, or a light shove would send her summersaulting into the abyss. She wished someone would push her. She dragged herself inside to an open seat as people cleared out at stops along the track and she collapsed exhausted. People stared at her puffy face, but she didn't care pulling the beret down around her ears and letting herself drift into a deep unconsciousness.

52

You have to live with yourself.

Lourdes, France

It felt like months since Letty left mother at the train station, but it was only a week. The train ride from Lyon to Lourdes was over 24 hours long, and she wanted it to be longer. She smoothed over the crumples of her dress as the train glided by houses on the outskirts of Lourdes. She adjusted her beret as they rolled into the station. Her calf muscles seized stepping down the stairs and she stopped before she got to the train platform. What did she need to say to convince mother to come with them?

Her eyes were bloodshot and she splashed water on her face in the station bathroom and applied some lipstick. Nothing she said to mother before about Switzerland registered. "It was a ridiculous idea." If she told her Suzy thought it was best for her to join, maybe that would convince her? "We want the family to stay together."

The air was cool and the early morning was black and thick with mist. The streets were quiet and only the light from the glow of street lamps dotted her path to mother. She counted them as she walked toward the hotel. She had the fleeting thought to walk to Nicholas's shop, but it was too early. He was sleeping, just like mother.

Letty turned the knob. Locked. She knocked and waited. Mother will think it's the *gendarmes* at this hour.

"Mother? It's me, Letty."

There was rustling and movement inside. Letty knew mother was a light sleeper, and was probably grabbing her robe. A latch was undone and the door opened. Blima stood there in her robe holding a hot stone wrapped in cloth for extra warmth. Letty noticed how grey her hair was and its short waves pressed back from her forehead. The wrinkles around her eyes and lips were always there, but she saw them more now. Her penetrating eyes were tired, and relieved to see her daughter. Mother hugged Letty before she entered the room.

"It's good to see you, Letty," she said. "What news do you have? Where are your sisters?"

"Annie and Suzy are in Aix-les-Bains waiting for us. How are you?"

"I've been spending time with that nice couple you met, Elijah and Rebecca. They're making plans and including me."

"Plans for what?" Letty said.

"For where to go next. Sit down Letty. Where are your things?"

"Mother, we have a good plan. Come with us. It's not safe in France. Annie barely escaped *razzias* in Marseille!"

"Is she okay?"

"Yes" Letty said nodding. "She's sick, but I think she's getting better. There was a *razzia* at the school she was staying and they took some children. Then in Marseille they blocked off an entire neighborhood while she was with the Lerners. She hid under a bed. It's not safe for us—"

"That's because you girls are putting yourself in harms way! If she stayed here that would've never happened!" She now spoke in Polish as opposed to Yiddish. Letty always knew her mood by the language she chose to speak. Yiddish was more proper, but when she was emotional and angry she spoke in Polish.

"Mother, it's not safe in France. Anywhere here. We need to leave. Come with me. Today. We're leaving."

"Did you get the French papers?" mother asked. Letty glanced down at her shoes avoiding mother's eyes. She didn't know how to tell her.

"A man made us papers in Marseille—"

"That's good!" mother said. Letty felt her throat seize up.

"But we couldn't get you one."

"Why?" Her face was disappointed, but not surprised.

"He needed you to be there."

"You expect me to travel over the border without proper papers?"

"There's no other choice."

"Why would I risk that, when you wouldn't?"

"You don't have to speak. We'll do all the talking."

"No, no. You're not serious. This is a terrible plan."

"There's a morning train. It's in a couple hours. Just pack your things and then you can decide. We'll take care of you." Mother scoffed at Letty.

"This is just another adventure for you. What will happen if they catch us? Have you thought about that? Tell me! You said it yourself! Look what happened to Annie in Marseille—"

"It can happen here! Anywhere in France! Where's safe in France? They'll catch us. This is our chance to get away." Mother shook her head not buying Letty's argument. Letty didn't think she took her daughters' proposal to escape seriously, for the simple reason that it came from Letty.

"I'll be better off here with my friends. Elijah has a plan and is including me. I knew you would abandon me. It's okay. You go." Mother inserted her words just under Letty's skin like a splinter. Letty's mouth was dry and no words came out for what seemed minutes. She avoided mother's hard stare looking around the barren room that had a well-used cot and a chair. Mother's clothes were folded in the corner and a dress hung on a hook.

"What's their plan?" Letty finally asked.

"We'll go to Nice." At the time Nice was in the Italian controlled zone and Jews were protected from the French and Germans.

"It's still France. Mother, France is not safe for Jews. You need to leave. If not with us, someone."

"Going on an escapade to Switzerland with no papers is safe?" Letty's temper tore at her chest like a jagged piece of broken-glass. She wanted to shake sense into her.

"Suzy thinks you should come with us."

"That's good for her. She's bought into your plan?"

"What about keeping the family together? We're going. Come with us so the family is together."

"You have all left me already. I've accepted that." Letty felt a heap of guilt slung on her shoulders and she retreated into her mind. She sat quiet for a while looking at the bare walls, the cracks in the plaster, the missing fixtures to calm herself.

"Have some food," mother said. Letty ripped off a chunk of baguette mother handed her. It was from earlier and a bit stale. "If you must go, you must. I will be okay."

Next to mother's bed was the book of Jewish love stories she read Letty when she was a girl. They weren't stories Letty thought about much, but the page was turned to Letty's favorite story about Adam's demonic ex-wife, Lilith. As a girl the story scared her. Before Eve came from Adam's rib, Lilith was Adam's wife, but demanded to be seen as his equal.

When Lilith was told she would always be Adam's inferior, she fled to live with demons. She tormented Adam and his family. There was a part of mother that feared Lilith's evil liberation. But it was ironic that mother also feared Eve, the apple of knowledge and being cast out of Eden. For her, there was no good ending either way.

"Do you need to leave?" mother asked. Letty did. "I'll walk you to the train station."

They didn't say a word as they looped through the downtown shops and shopkeepers swept the street, getting ready for morning business. When they arrived at the station there were a few people scattered along the platform. Letty stood there waiting for mother to change her mind. But she was quiet. Letty looked at her to see if there was any change.

"Please take a chance with us. You don't have to talk. We'll do all the talking. We have a plan. Trust us."

"I don't feel safe making this trip."

"Mother, please come with us." As the train was pulling into the station, each plea for her to come became half-hearted, and Letty felt a twinge in her stomach. Part of her hoped she refused. It's not a nice thought, but it was the truth. Deep down she knew if mother came, there was little chance they'd make it into Switzerland. Mother became hysterical in stressful situations. Without wanting to, she would betray them. The more Letty thought she didn't want her to come, the more she urged her to go. "Come with us. There is nothing for us in France. You only need to step out of your comfort zone one more time."

"No, I'll stay." Letty didn't pretend to be upset, but the calm sense of relief set in. It was with guilt and sadness that she wrapped her arms around mother. She squeezed her not wanting to let go of her familiarity, her smell, and the rigid firmness of her back. Letty pulled away and saw her tight lips. If she had the passport would she have agreed to come, and if she had a smuggler would that have made a difference? Letty waited for her to change her mind. Mother blinked, but said nothing.

Letty stepped on the first stair of the train nervous and waiting for mother to say something, waiting for her to trust her daughters and join them, waiting for her to yell at Letty to get her things. Letty looked over her shoulder and felt butterflies in her stomach. Mother watched her find a seat through the train windows. Her mouth was an even line, her eyes fierce like when Letty was a child. But she stood alone on the train platform afraid of the future. Afraid of being someone she wasn't. Afraid of change. It was just fear. Her mouth opened a hair and she breathed as if she was going to speak. Did she change her mind? It closed.

Letty tried to read her face, to understand how she let her children leave without her. She was thankful mother let them go, but angry that she didn't trust her at the same time. Was it an easy decision? Were Elijah and Rebecca so much more reliable than her daughters that she chose them? How could she let them go? They made it this far, why not a little further? Did she let Letty leave because she didn't want to burden them? Did she let them go so they could escape? Or was she just tired of running?

Letty was relieved, but soaked in shame. She was leaving her mother behind.

The land outside moved and the station and her mother slipped away. Her ears were wringing preventing Letty from hearing if mother was yelling for her to stop and to jump off the train. She tried harder to listen and then looked back. Mother stood in the noise of the spewing railcars in solemn silence with her fingers clasped together. She also looked at peace.

The train ride back to Lyon and Aix-les-Bains was a blur of emotions. Letty tried to make sense of it all but was unable to hear her thoughts or anyone. She remembered handing a conductor a handful of money for the ticket and him giving change. Faceless people sat down next to her and got up. She stared into the French countryside and it faded into dusk and then nothing but pitch black. The noise of the rails rattled in her head like a metronome numbing her to the melody of life that was happening around her.

53

Resist the trap of presuming others know the way.

Aix-les-Bains, France

In Aix-les-Bains, almost three days after Letty left Suzy and Annie in Lyon, the breeze swept off Lake Bourget into the quiet city. The only things moving were sailboats in the harbor, rubbing against moorings in the early morning.

Outside the train station was a hotel that was an obvious choice for her sisters, but they weren't there when Letty checked. There was another hotel nearby. Letty headed for it trying to put her mother out of her head. It was time to focus.

"Is there an Annie or Suzy Schmidt staying here?" she asked. The concierge flipped through a book of occupants.

"There's no one by that name staying with us," the man said looking at his guest list. Letty's quickened breathing turned into full-blown panic as she walked out of the hotel and into the morning light. Did they even come to Aix-les-Bains? Did something happen to them? Why didn't they have a better plan? Then she realized the problem and went back inside.

"How about Rene and Antoinette Picard?" He looked through his book again.

"They are on the second floor."

When the door opened a man was standing there.

"Can I help you?" he said.

"I think I have the wrong room."

"No, no," Suzy said from inside the room. "Letty, we're here."

She saw Annie and Suzy stare to see if mother was coming behind her, but the man closed the door.

"They're leaving tomorrow for Switzerland," Suzy said as Letty set her bag down, referring to the two boys in the room. "They have a smuggler, Letty. We should have gotten a smuggler." Suzy and Annie met the two brothers from Antwerp on the train from Lyon and they offered to pay for the room.

"Mother didn't come with you?" Annie said after they sat in silence for several minutes.

"No."

"It was because we didn't have a smuggler or papers for her," Suzy said.

"I don't know."

"Did you tell her we'd speak for her?" Annie said.

"Yes."

"Was it the passport?"

"I don't know, probably."

"She would have come if we had a smuggler," Suzy said. The two men sat like spectators.

Letty felt her mother abandoned the family for better prospects. But she was conflicted, because by not joining them she gave them a better chance to get across. Letty struggled to get those thoughts out of her head so she could start planning the border crossing.

First they needed to get to Annemasse, the spot Nicholas pointed at on the map. The Vichy and Nazis were clamping down on the borders and snatching Jews trying to escape. The Nazis instituted the 'J' stamp for Jews, and required the Swiss to turn the Jews they caught over to them. Perhaps it was Suzy's constant needling, but

Letty was becoming worried they didn't have a smuggler.

She watched Suzy strike up a conversation with one of the brothers in the corner. She kept her voice low, yet Letty still overheard her. Eli was the older one and Natan was his younger brother who followed everything Eli said. Suzy focused her efforts on Eli.

"Who's taking you over?" Suzy said. She grabbed a brush and ran it through her hair.

"A man we met at a camp in Marseille."

"You can trust him?"

"He was recommended by family. He helped them get to Switzerland."

"Could he help us?" She stopped brushing her hair.

"Yes, come with us."

"How much is it?"

"4,000 Francs."

"For two?"

"For one."

"That's 8,000 for both of you? We don't have that type of money."

"Yes, it was most of the money we had. Our family will pay the rest from Switzerland."

"Could they help us? Pay for us?"

"I don't know if our family could afford three—"

Suzy's lips were moving, but Letty didn't make it out. What did she say?

54

Blend in and observe.

Annemasse, France

Annemasse was on the border of Switzerland en route to Geneva, Switzerland. It was still part of the Vichy controlled zone, which meant there weren't Nazi guards, only French *gendarmes*. Bousquet increased his patrols on the borders where refugees crossed, and on the other side, Swiss police were also patrolling for refugees and turning any Jewish captives over to the French and Germans. The Swiss refused to grant entry visas to Jewish refugees above the age of 16. Those arrested in Switzerland went straight to the concentration camps back in France.

When Letty woke in the morning her eyes shot open and she saw the empty boys' bed. They already left for the border. Her head snapped up, searching for Suzy. She was gone too.

The door opened.

"I got the name and contact of the smuggler," Suzy said as she closed the door behind her.

Letty didn't know if she was trying to put the pressure on, or simply being helpful, so she ignored her comment, choosing instead to focus on the task at hand.

"I'm going go to Annemasse today to scout where we cross," Letty said. It was Letty's plan and she didn't even know where they were going.

She grabbed her new passport, a coat and put on the beret. Letty knew by the clothes and the faces in the train car to Annemasse that it was filled with refugees staring at the passing countryside in silence. If she could tell, so could the *gendarmes*.

When the train arrived in Annemasse, it was pouring rain. She hid in a corridor of the station trying to get her bearings and work her courage up to explore the area for crossing routes. She didn't have a clue about where to go or even how to sneak over the border. Stepping out from underneath the eves of the station and into the pelting rain she covered her head with a jacket, keeping close to the shops. On a corner was a church.

"You can always trust a believer," mother once said to Letty when they rode in a horse-cart between Bojanow and Ranizow in Poland. Letty saw a man crossing himself with his right hand as he passed the church.

She surveyed the church in Annemasse, remembering mother's words and her solemn stare. Pulling the heavy church door open, the musky dampness wafted out. The wood benches were empty as was the hall. There were tapestries embroidered with The Stations of the Cross on the walls.

"Hello," Letty said, nervous to disturb the religious inhabitants. Her voice echoed and she shivered. From the back a man emerged in a black cloak and white collar. At the front of the church was what she realized was Jesus on the cross. Her stomach twisted at the thought of Mr. Lerner's boy and his Jesus joke years earlier during Purim dinner. If there was a God, he heard it.

"It's quite wet outside," the priest said as he walked through the pews. "What brings you to us today?"

"I'm a refugee looking to get across the border." She looked at his face for signs he might go to the authorities. He studied her shoes and clothes, but was silent as he clasped his hands together. "My sisters and I don't know where to go. Do you know where one might cross into Switzerland?"

"I've heard that Saint Julien is the best place." There was no hesitation in his voice.

"Where is that?"

"It's very simple. It's 20 minutes down the road. Come." He gestured for Letty to follow him outside. They went to the sidewalk and the rain had let up to a slight mist. "Go that way. There are open stretches of the border." The priest pointed into the far-off horizon.

"Thank you—"

"Friend!" the Priest yelled. A motorcycle drove by and the priest put his arm up waving him over.

"Hello, Father!" Before the man took his helmet off the priest put his hand on his arm.

"Can you help this girl with a ride to Saint Julien?"

"Sure, Father."

"He will take you."

"Thank you, Father," Letty said.

She climbed onto the back of the motorcycle and put her arms around the man's waist. She'd never been on a motorcycle before. He revved the engine and they took off down a back road. Her hair whipped and she grabbed her beret before it flew off with one hand, and clutched the driver for dear life with the other. They zipped passed farms, around cows standing in the road and by farmers driving horse-carts filled with hay.

"Where you going?" he said over the hum of the engine.

"I don't know!" she said.

"I'll drop you off in the center of Saint Julien."

Letty expected to see a fence, a barrier, or some sort of demarcation, but there was nothing when the motorcyclist dropped her off. It was then Letty realized she didn't know what a border looked like. They were just lines on her map. Finding the actual country of Switzerland proved a little more challenging, and even more so, locating the place they could get across where there were no police.

A coffee shop was nestled in the town center and Letty settled in with a newspaper to observe. The priest was sure the best border crossing was near here. So she stayed put. It was like being in one of the spy movies she watched in Antwerp. She sipped coffee, warming her hands on the mug as she glanced at the newspaper and then at patrons for clues. Even their faces, their shoes, their conversations, and their mannerisms might provide some clues. She waited an hour and nothing appeared helpful for her mission. People came and left and she wondered if it was a waste of time. Her focus kept coming back to two men who had been at their table for a while. Then two women joined them and they all laughed at a joke. Letty crossed them off her mental list of possible leads.

Huddled in the corner was a man that looked Jewish. It was his hair and facial features. The way he gestured with his hands. He seemed familiar to Letty, like he was from her neighborhood in Antwerp. He was bent over a table talking to another man who didn't look Jewish at all. His nose was sharp and hair blond. "I bet this was a smuggler and a refugee." They were in a quiet discussion, almost a whisper. She looked at her newspaper not wanting to attract attention and became conscious of how much she glanced over. Butterflies fluttered in her belly. This had to be a smuggler.

They talked and seemed to be waiting. It was getting dark outside and they pushed back from the table and put their jackets on. Her stomach swirled. This was her chance. She drank her coffee and let them leave the café. They walked by the window before she even got up. When she closed the door behind her they were down the street and making a right at the corner.

One block turned into two and then three and still they walked. Their pace was fast, but not rushed. The shops gave way to fields and some industrial land and train depots. Abandoned railcars rusted in fields and stacks of pilings sat in high grass. They stayed on the road, their pace quickening. Her short legs did their best to keep up, but she stayed back. Then she worried they'd disappear. It was dusk and the shadows were giving way to night. There was also the possibility this was a wild goose chase, yet her gut said to follow.

Up ahead Letty watched them walk by an open field and the Gentile nodded his head. The Jewish man ran through the high grass and disappeared into the woods. There was a rustle in the distance and the snapping of branches, but the man didn't come back. The Gentile man stopped and turned back toward Letty. He came close to her inspecting who she was.

"Is it true the border is here?" Letty asked. He looked at her and shrugged like he didn't know what she was talking about. "What does the border look like?" Letty still thought it was some sort of wall she had to climb over.

"What do you mean, girl?"

"Is there a big barbed-wire fence or wall?"

"Oh, you just cross the railroad track and you're in Switzerland."

"That's interesting," she said. She could hardly contain her excitement. The man kept walking and turned up another road vanishing before she asked any more questions. Letty stared at the spot taking a mental picture and hoped the Jewish man didn't spend a lot of money for the Gentile to nod his head at this field.

55

Wave like you're on an evening stroll.

Saint Julien, France

"I've found our place to cross!" Letty said, after she entered their room and closed the door. "We need to go."

She looked at the beaten suitcases, with scuffs and cuts in the leather. They each had a bag filled with clothes, which were heavy to carry to a train station, let alone across the border, especially if they had to run.

"We'll have to get rid of these," she said kicking her suitcase. "Take only one for the three of us. These will be too heavy to carry."

"What about clothes?" Suzy said. "We'll need something."

"Throw them away," she said. Letty looked at Annie's feet, already rubbed raw from the wood shoes she wore. Leather shoes were impossible to obtain now that armies were taking every scrap for soldiers' boots.

"What about this?" Annie said holding up the alarm clock.

"Take the money out and get rid of it," Suzy said. "It's needless weight." When Suzy turned around to dump her fine dresses on the floor, Annie put it under the clothes in the one bag they were taking.

The rain pattered throughout the night, pounding at times. The next morning the rain continued to pour and dark clouds hung low like night never left.

When Letty took the heaps of extra clothes and suitcases to the trash outside in the alley there was a newspaper laying at the front door of the building, stopping her in her tracks. She picked it up. "Police Arrest Refugees Attempting to Cross Border in Saint Julien," was the headline. "Oh, no." This was an ominous sign. Thoughts flew through her head. Were they about to walk into a trap?

She dropped the paper. "The hell with it, if they arrested someone yesterday, it was unlikely they'd arrest someone today." The die was cast and she left their suitcases next to the trash bin.

Letty didn't dare tell her sisters about the newspaper headline. Nothing good came from trying to cross the border with terrified sisters. Instead she led the way carrying the bag to the train station, with Annie clip-clopping in her wood shoes behind Suzy.

Not one person uttered a word in the passenger car; only sniffles and the rustle of jackets were heard. It may have been nerves, but Letty sat frozen, going over the newspaper article. Was she dragging her sisters into a trap? She fought against the agonizing thoughts until they were out of her head.

The rain didn't let up in Saint Julien and their coats and berets were dripping. Letty brought them to the same café as the day before. She looked at the round tables and some familiar faces in the café. They bought coffees and sat hunched over the steaming cups waiting and warming their bodies. She wondered about the Jewish man yesterday. Did he make it? Was he one of those caught?

They were on the edge of the border about to go for it. She looked at her sisters' wet faces and hair. They placed a lot of faith in her. Letty took a deep breath.

"Are you okay?" Suzy asked. "Is something wrong?"

"No, nothing is wrong," Letty said and sipped her coffee.

It needed to be dark to have the best chance not to get pinched by border guards. The streetlights came on. Maybe the rain would stop. Letty second-guessed the crossing point and her memory and wished they had a smuggler. She didn't know if she could find the spot in the pouring rain. It was a pitch-black night. Out the window sheets of

WAVE LIKE YOU'RE ON AN EVENING STROLL.

rain pelted the road with no sign it was letting up.

"When do we leave?" Suzy said.

"When it's dark," Letty said in a whisper.

"It's dark." Buildings and the road disappeared outside in the rain and clouds soaked up almost every bit of light cast by the street lamps, leaving only a couple faint dots in the night.

"Let's go then," Letty said, choking on the words stuck in her throat.

The rain flew in the door and they were drenched in seconds. Letty headed in the direction where she thought the Jewish man and smuggler went the day before, but now she was turned around by the night and heavy weather. The beating patter of rain was all she heard. There was a building on the left she didn't remember seeing. This wasn't the way. Maybe she didn't notice it before? Letty wiped the water from her eyes and stopped.

"I can't see the path I found yesterday," she said. "We have to find another way." Panic pulsed into every limb of her body. She didn't know which direction it was to the border and her brain seized up, unable to make a decision about where to go. Water streamed down and her eyes were blinded by the amount of water pelting into her face.

"Mother always said, 'Turn to the right,'" Annie said.

There was no logical reason for it, but so it was decided. They took the next "turn to the right" and onto a dark street. In the distance there was a light moving in the rain and getting closer. Border guards? As the glow got bigger Letty realized that three girls walking along the border in the rain at this time of night was suspicious.

The beam of light turned into a dark figure with an umbrella and flashlight now twenty feet from them.

"Are you lost?" a voice said from the blackness. The sheets of rain continued to pound down.

As the figure approached Letty saw his face in the glow of the flashlight. His cheeks were wet and the shadows highlighted the wrinkles around his jowls. His face was kind.

"Hello, *monsieur*," Letty said. "We're Jewish refugees trying to get across the border. Can you point us the way."

"Letty, watch what you say," Suzy said in Flemish under her breath. "You'll get us arrested."

"Oui, *mes enfants*," the old man said. He pointed to a building by the railroad crossing. "There's a woman that changes the tracks, the switcher. Go to her."

He shined his light at the wood-sided building down the road so they knew for sure which one he meant.

"*Merci*," Letty said.

Letty started walking and Suzy and Annie hung back not sure if it was a good idea. Through the window was an old woman wearing a billed hat and overalls, brewing up some hot water on a potbelly stove. Letty tapped her knuckles on the door and the woman opened it. Her face was sour like she was disturbed from important business.

"A man sent us here," Letty said. "We're Jewish refugees trying to get across the border." She examined the soaked clothes. There was warmth from her stove that touched Letty's face.

"Wait here," she said closing the door, leaving Letty to the elements. Letty saw through the windows as the woman check outside. Was she looking for the police? It was a long couple of minutes as she stood in the rain. Letty peered back at her sisters who were ten feet behind and didn't know what was going on. The tips of her fingers tingled and she rubbed her hands together. Letty leaned in to see what the woman was up to, but fogged up the window with her breath. The door opened.

"Go across the tracks to that building," she said pointing to a house no more than twenty yards away across the railway. "There's a patrol of *gendarmes* walking the rails. They passed minutes ago. Watch out. Tell her I sent you."

Letty waved her sisters to follow and they stepped over the rails and wood pilings. The house was close, yet as fast as they walked it seemed to take forever to cover the ground in between.

"Who goes there!" a man shouted from behind as they crossed the last train track. They were yards from the house and they looked back to see what was likely two *gendarmes* waving and walking down the railway toward them. Letty waved to them. "The border is this way!" a *gendarme* said from a distance of about five boxcars, waving them back over.

Letty was confused and trying to understand what was going on. They flipped on their flashlights shining them and calling them over. Were they in Switzerland?

"You're going the wrong way!" one *gendarme* yelled. They were in rain gear and Letty didn't know if they were Swiss or French.

"The police are coming," Annie said. "Are we in Switzerland?"

"I don't know," Letty said.

Did they need to show their passports to pass? Letty remembered the smuggler telling her the border was over the tracks. She looked down at the ground to make sure they were over.

"You're going the wrong way!" he yelled again.

Letty casually waved back and headed to the house, knocking on the door.

She tried the door again as the *gendarme* came closer. It opened and a woman stood there with a lamp.

"The switch woman sent us," Letty said.

"You want to pass?" she said.

"Yes."

The woman grabbed her arm and pulled her inside. Annie and Suzy were quick to follow. The *gendarme* stood watching from across the tracks. With a flurry of instructions, the woman led them winding through her house while they dripped on her wood floors all the way to the back door. She opened it and pointed.

"Keep your back to the mountain," she said waving her hands in so many directions Letty didn't keep track. "Geneva is that way. As long as you walk with your back to the mountain, you'll get there. Look for the city lights. Don't let the Swiss police catch you. Not around here."

"So we're in Switzerland?" Annie said.

"Yes," she said. "You are."

With those instructions they set off into the rain again. It was so dark and rainy Letty was unable to see the path. To get their bearings Suzy kneeled down and lit a match under her coat and cradled it with her hand. That one cardboard stick illuminated the night for miles it seemed. It burned until it scorched her fingers and she threw it into the mud. Letty located the mountain, Mont Saleve, and they walked in the opposite direction away from France.

The rain was so unrelenting that she only guessed the mountain was behind them and they weren't circling back into France, but she didn't know. They trudged through the sloppy mud, which clung to their feet and ankles.

The mud got worse the further they trod. Annie's feet were torn and bleeding from the wooden shoes. The thick, deep goo pulled at them with each step and they fought for their next. One of Annie's wood shoes was sucked off and disappeared into the slop. She walked on with one bare foot.

"What are we to do when we get to the city?" Annie said. "I have one shoe. We'll be spotted."

Through the rain they saw a small farmhouse ahead. As they walked towards it flashlights bounced in the distance. Two lights. They were coming their direction from beyond the farmhouse.

"Let's ask them for help," Annie said. "Hello!" Her yell broke over the pounding of the rain.

"No, no, Annie," Letty said.

"Shush," Suzy said putting her hand over Annie's mouth to silence her.

"We don't know who it is," Letty said. The lights were getting closer as they approached the farm. "The barn." They tugged open the barn door and crouched inside an empty horse stall. There were two horses in the other stalls. Peering through the slats of the barn wall they watched the lights get brighter. Letty's breathing slowed as the beams flitted over the mud showing the divots from their feet.

It was two Swiss policemen with dogs and Letty held her breath.

234

Their voices carried through the night, muffled by the rain and dampness. The dogs pulled them forward as their boots sloshed through the mud.

"It's police," Annie said in a whisper. Suzy put her hand over Annie's mouth squeezing her lips.

They were no more than five yards away as they walked by wearing ponchos. One of their German Shepherds looked at the barn and woofed. Not a full bark. More of a bark that was unsure of what it smelled, but the horses stirred in their stalls and the Swiss police kept walking. Letty was now thankful for the rain and the mud and the disorder of the night.

"Who's there?" A man's voice demanded from outside the barn. They crouched lower not saying a word. "I said, 'who's there?'"

Letty watched the bouncing glow of the police down the hill. Letty guessed it was the farmer checking on his horses and she didn't want to give him reason to get the police.

"We're refugees from France," she said. "We'll leave." He was silent for a moment.

"Stay until it's safe," he said. "If the police catch you they'll turn you over to the French." That was all he said and they heard the bang of a house door close. They waited, hugging each other for warmth as the cold air burrowed through their wet clothes like an ice conductor, and their body temperatures dropped. They had to keep moving, and left the barn.

The rain was letting up and Letty made out the mountain to their backs. They were going the opposite direction of the Swiss patrol. The moon and stars broke through the heavy night clouds revealing that they were covered in mud. Not just their shoes and legs, but their dresses were brown, hair filled with slime, and faces streaked. They were a mess.

"We can't walk into Geneva like this," Annie said. She was right.

Dogs barked as they passed farms, and people were sleeping. Ahead on a knoll was a home with lights still on.

56

A warm hearth will warm the heart.

Geneva, Switzerland

Letty approached the sturdy oak door. Her sisters stood shivering a safe distance away outside the gate. Smoke came from the chimney and a dog inside howled letting their presence be known before she knocked. An older man in a hairy sweater opened the door and right behind him a woman poked her head out.

"Good evening," Letty said. "We crossed the border from France and have been walking all night. We're refugees. Can you take us in?" He looked at her, and then over at her sisters.

"Of course, children," he said. "Come in, come in."

"I'll heat water for baths," his wife said throwing wood onto the fire.

The warmth of the fire radiated off Letty's face. They stood watching these two people open their home to three muddy girls from the night. While her husband fetched more water from a well outside to pour into a caldron sitting on the blazing fire, she pulled out a meat pie filled with beef, mushrooms and a creamy sauce. If the pie wasn't enough she presented fresh loaves of Bürli, small breads, that was probably for their morning breakfast.

"Wash up, my dears," She said. "Then you can eat." The woman led them to a room wallpapered with flowers where her husband had a tub of steaming water waiting. She brought an armful of crisp, clean clothes. "Here are some of my dresses you can have, and a pair of shoes for you." She handed them to Annie.

It was like a dream Letty never wanted to wake up from. After washing up, Letty put on the starchy clean flower print dress that smelled of the sun. It was the first new clothes she had received in years. By the time they sat at the table to eat Letty felt like a different person. The wood paneled walls of the house were filled with pictures of children, and the mantle had ceramic figurines of cows, horses and decorative plates.

The woman flitted about and didn't say much except, "eat your food while it's hot; give me your dirty clothes; there are blankets if you are cold; is there anything else you need?" She must have missed her children. Her husband was content to sit in his overstuffed, red, upholstered chair by the fire and wait for orders from his wife.

When they were done eating the hot, delicious meat pie, the woman took the three of them to a room. "I'm sorry, but there are only two beds," she said. "My boys shared this room." Annie and Letty climbed into one bed, Suzy went to the other and the woman tucked them in as if they were her children. She watched them from the door as they slipped into a deep slumber.

In the morning they were woken by the smell of coffee and warm bread with honey. The woman was washing the dishes from the night before and her husband brought wood in from the shed.

"Eat the food before it gets cold," she said.

"What's the best way to Geneva?" Letty asked.

"There's a street car a few miles up that will take you downtown," he said. "Do you have money?"

"We have French Francs," she said.

"Here's enough to get you to Geneva," he said handing her money. "You can exchange your money once you're there. Try to get far from the border and Geneva. They'll turn you over to the Gestapo."

With the woman's clean clothes on their backs and full bellies they headed toward Geneva up the dirt road, navigating around deep ruts of mud to a station.

Geneva sits on an expansive lake cutting into the Alps for as far as the eye can see. The streetcar weaved through tight streets down to the lake.

"Where are we going?" Annie asked. It hadn't been discussed. Only getting into Switzerland. Now that they were inside, they didn't know where to go.

"Zurich," Suzy said. Getting far away from the French border and Geneva was all that mattered. Without further discussion they bought three tickets to Zurich handing Swiss Francs to a station booking clerk. It wasn't until Letty was in her seat and the engine tugged them out of the station that she unfolded her map. That was when she saw how close Zurich was to the German border.

57

Only in a race is there a finish line.

Zurich, Switzerland

Letty was just getting her bearings outside the train station in Zurich, a massive sandstone baroque palace, when two boys in their twenties pointed at them and whispered to each other. Did Letty know them? She didn't recognize them. They sat on the fountain staring.

Near the two boys were older men hovering. One man sitting near the boys looked away when she noticed him. He wore a jacket, sunglasses, and collared shirt. Another stood by holding a newspaper.

"Hello, Annie!" one of the boys said waving his arm. "It's Braun from Antwerp!"

"Oh, wow, I know them," Annie said to Letty in a low voice. "They are brothers from Mrs. Ostersetzer's class. Hello, Braun! Hello, Falek!" Annie said waving and yelling. The men sitting near in plainclothes descended on Letty and her sisters from all directions, even from behind.

"Police!" they said. "Come with us." It happened so fast Letty was shocked. They made it all the way and the police caught her ten steps outside the finish line. It was unbelievable.

With firm grips on their arms they led the girls to the underbelly and holding cells. The rooms were dark under the Prussian train station. Letty looked at the men smoking cigarettes and eyeing them as they wrote up their reports. All of Letty's documents were spread out on the desk as they entered her names. She didn't know what they were going to do with them. Turn them over to the French, the Germans? They were now closer to the German border. It was less than a 40-minute drive.

A man came out of a room wearing a turtleneck shirt and blazer. His blonde hair hid the greys of his age and was slicked over to the side. The other men greeted him with reverence. He was the man in charge.

"What do we have here?" he said in German. Letty understood enough German to make out what they said.

"We picked them up outside the station along with a couple boys we were watching, sir," the man said. He scribbled down in his reports. "Jewish refugees, I think. What do you want us to do?"

"You can make these calls," the boss said. "I told you before. I don't have to be the one to make these decisions. I've given you authority to do so." The man looked up from the paperwork, and his stare was blank. The boss shook his head, now annoyed and picked up the paperwork, thumbing through it.

"You," the boss said in French pointing at Suzy. "Come with me." He led her into a room. Suzy was gone twenty minutes before the boss emerged with her. He seated her on the other side of the room away from her sisters. Letty looked at Suzy studying her face. She didn't look at her. Were her eyes red from tears, or just tired?

"Your turn," he said to Annie. Annie disappeared through the metal door. She was gone longer than Suzy. She must have had more to say. Then she reemerged her eyes wet from tears. The boss man in his turtleneck pointed at Annie to sit a couple seats away from Suzy, "Here." He pointed at Letty and curled his finger, telling her to follow. She sensed he didn't like his job, and she knew he held her fate in his hands.

"Take a seat," he said in French, but with a harsh German accent. He closed the door with a soft touch. There was a metal table that looked as if it belonged in a butcher shop. He sat across from Letty and she smelled what he had for lunch, sausages.

"State your name," he said.

"Marie Picard," she said.

"Well, that's funny. It says Zlata Schmidt from Antwerp, here on this document. Which is it?" He thumbed through Letty's documents and slid over a statement by her sisters. "Nothing is accomplished here with games."

"My given name is Zlata. But they call me Letty."

"Okay, that's better. Where are you from?"

"Antwerp. But we came over from France." She didn't mention she was born in Berlin.

"What are you doing in Switzerland?"

"My sisters crossed over the border from France a couple days ago."

"Where?"

"Saint Julien."

"Who helped you?" Letty thought of the woman who let them walk through her house on the border, the farmer that let them hide in his barn, and the nice couple that took them in.

"No one, really. Some farmers gave us food and clean clothes. I don't remember their names—"

"You just walked over here from France? Three girls?"

"Yes sir."

"Are you Jewish?" Letty hesitated to answer. It was common knowledge they were hunting Jews and turning them over to the Nazis. "Are you?" he asked again.

"Yes," she said.

"The regulations of my job require me to turn you over to French authorities. You crossed over from France." He looked at the papers spread out on the desk. He was mulling over their future. "In August the government stated that Jews are not political refugees. I repeat. Jews are not political refugees. Our laws say political refugees won't be expelled from our borders. I see that you have spent only a day in Switzerland. Do you understand? You are Jewish, not a political prisoner. Therefore I'm instructed by Swiss law to turn you over."

She nodded, seeing the power he held with his decision.

"Do I have any reason to believe you're a political refugee?"

"Yes," she said. "Yes."

"Jews aren't political refugees. You heard me just say that?"

"Yes." What other option did she have?

"Are you still claiming you're a political refugee?"

Letty nodded.

"I need proof," he said. "Your sisters gave me no proof." Her mind was seizing up. She didn't know political things. She had never been political, but she thought about Antwerp. Somehow the boy who once chased her down an alley popped into her head and how he yelled at her. She didn't forget his snarl. "Do you have proof?" His eyes pleaded with her.

"The Flemish National League in Belgium persecuted us for having no Flanders heritage," she said. She didn't know how it sounded, but the newspapers in Belgium talked about it. She never gave it much thought until the boy chased her. The officer looked at her. In his eyes he didn't want to turn them over to the Germans or the French. He started writing in the files in front of him. He got up and left the room.

Letty knew he needed to check her story. There wasn't much she could do now and in that moment she was at peace with either outcome. She did everything in her power. The metal door opened again and the officer stood in front of her.

"Today is your lucky day. You need to file with the Jewish Community Organization in Lavaterstrasse as soon as you leave. They will help you. Or you'll be picked up again and sent out of Switzerland. Understand?"

He ushered her out giving the stack of reports back to the man at the desk. Suzy and Annie stared at her as the officer disappeared behind another door. The man at the desk looked at the reports and his boss's signatures. He gathered their passports, money, bag, and handed them back. A plain-clothed officer stood up and opened the door back through the underbelly of the train station into the light of Zurich.

58

One piece of information can change your life.

Switzerland was an important center for espionage and the Nazis and Allied countries brokered deals in the dark rooms of alehouses. German officers on leave from the war strolled through the shops and cafes in Zurich dressed up in their grey uniforms and tall black boots.

Letty and her sisters reported to Zurich's Jewish Community Organization and stayed in a small room with their support. There was a Gentile in her late twenties that lived there and smoked on the building's front steps every afternoon after she woke, her eyes still groggy and filled with mascara from the night before. Letty avoided her most days. She always looked as if she'd snap if you spoke to her.

Letty stepped around her like a cat, but one day she put her hand out with a cigarette, offering one before Letty slipped by.

"*Merci*," Letty said. She took the cigarette and sat next to her and the girl struck a match and lit it. It was the first time Letty smoked. Even though the girl's hair was matted from her pillow she was pretty. Her eyes were still crusted with sleep.

"I need to leave for work in a little," she said. "I see you girls. You're new here." Letty nodded as she puffed on the cigarette.

"Where do you work?" Letty said caressing the thin cigarette between her two fingers and inhaling the smoke. It was smooth and

243

tasted good.

"At a nightclub," she said. "I'm a dancer."

Letty inhaled and nodded.

"Are you a refugee?"

"From France. How did you know?"

"By the way you're dressed. Your accent. You know?" she said as she stared at the street. "These German officers tell me some terrible things at the club. Some are bragging and some clearing their conscience. They tell me all sorts when they're drunk."

Letty didn't say anything, but looked at the dress the nice farm lady gave her, and the shoes she wore. She tried to clean the mud off, but they were well worn and dirty. It was easy for the police to spot her as an outsider.

"They have these ovens," she said, "and they're putting people in the ovens at the camps. All the Jews. Annihilating them."

Letty's heart lodged in her throat. She didn't expect to hear those words. Not from this girl. It was the way she said it. The woman was calm, but she had to tell someone, just as the soldier who told her had to tell someone. It wasn't something she could keep to herself. It was how she said it that Letty knew it was true. She instantly thought of father and the last time she saw him during Purim in Antwerp, and mother, left behind in France. Letty felt ill.

59

The self-righteous need to have fun.

Adliswil, Switzerland

Swiss authorities came to the apartments and notified Letty and her sisters that they were being placed into a military camp in the small town of Adliswil, just outside of Zurich. Trucks filled with Jews transported them out of the city. They were separated from the men and marched with women to barracks with wood partitions and straw scattered on the floor. The Jewish men were sent to labor camps. It was forbidden to leave the camp, and only one hour a day were they allowed to walk around the grounds.

As a show of force the captain of the camp called the women into the parade yard and they stood in the brisk wind huddling close together for warmth. A barrack door swung open and two guards led out a girl Letty recognized from her neighborhood in Antwerp. She was brought in front of the women, standing next to the captain, a short man with trimmed hair. He put his spectacles on and read her offenses in a loud voice.

"For the violation of the correspondence law, which is strictly forbidden by rule, the violator will serve three days of confinement for attempting to send a letter," the captain read in French, his voice rigid as he pronounced the words with a Swiss accent showing his proclivity for German. "All laws of this camp must be obeyed to protect the security of the camp and Switzerland. Without compromise."

A guard grabbed the girl and pulled her out of the camp. This posed a problem for contacting mother.

Life was regimented and Letty worked in the kitchen washing pots and helping prepare lunch. It wasn't a bad place to be. The women were in good spirits and laughed. They showed her how to cook and made the best meals with the ingredients and spices they had. Women from all over Europe (Germany, Austria, France, Poland and Belgium), who managed to flee the Nazis, came together blending their culinary sensibilities. There was no kosher meat, but many non-Orthodox Jews ate the aromatic meals they prepared. While cutting carrots, peeling potatoes and boiling water the chatter didn't stop. It was here Letty learned that Rabbi Tauber from Zurich came to the camp once a week to check on conditions and brought kosher potatoes and pasta. He was the "connection" to the outside world.

Letty (right) works in a refugee camp kitchen.

Rabbi Tauber was an unassuming man and had eyes that took in every detail as they flitted from side to side. Women needled him for information about other camps, their families, and news about the war. He was a popular man.

When he came through the barracks with bags stuffed with blankets, they took several. It was getting cold, but Letty was also told this was how you passed information to him. Suzy pressed a letter into his hand as she grabbed a blanket. He didn't acknowledge it, just tucked it away in his big overcoat, which was bulging with other pieces of mail.

In the letter Annie wrote mother how to get a smuggler. They had a good contact through the boys Suzy met in Aix-les-Bains and money to pay for her through a Jewish organization. "Please make the trip and join us in Switzerland," Annie wrote. She addressed the envelope and Suzy signed it. Now they waited to hear from her.

It was a blustering October and frigid air streamed through the boards of the barracks and its high-pitch whistle hurt the ears. Suzy and Annie took the extra blankets and hung them on the walls to block the wind and decorate. The blankets were colorful patterns of reds, yellows and greens. They brightened the dreariness of the barrack.

They also used them to silence their cranky wall mate, an old German woman on the other side of their partition. If they spoke to each other Mrs. Karpiniski complained about the noise. When they giggled, she yelled at them, "quiet down." When they moved in their little space she grumbled about the racket they made. "Nothing but chaos over there. Will they ever settle down? They've kept me up day and night."

It was a day like all the rest when the captain of the camp walked through the barrack inspecting for infractions and tidiness. He stopped in front of their living space, staring at the blankets on the wall and their family photos of mother and father arranged around the small hay stall. Letty didn't know if he was about to march them into the parade field for violating a code.

"Hmmm, interesting," he said. He stepped inside for a better look, his hands clasped behind his back. Her heart beat fast. "A functional use that brings hominess to the barracks. This is wonderful. I would like others to see this." He called other women in the barrack to see. "Ladies! Step over here!" Women gathered outside and poked their heads in. "This is a model room. Please take note."

"Captain, I'll have you know they make awful racket," Mrs. Karpiniski said from the other side of the partition. "I don't need to come by to know that. Please have them respect other people's quiet." He looked at them, and so did the other women. Letty wanted to tell that dreary lady she wished the Nazis got her, but she bit her tongue and felt bad about the thought.

The captain ignored the woman and continued his inspection as the other women filtered back to their living areas snickering at the old lady's jest. "Those Schmidt girls are loud."

Suzy pulled mother's alarm clock out and wound it.

"Does this still work?" she said. She set the time for hours later into the middle of the night and its quiet monotonous tick wasn't even heard over their breaths. Suzy put the alarm clock behind her back. They heard the cantankerous neighbor shuffle by and she even sneered, with her dark eyes receded into her head, as she followed others out to eat. Her skin draped over her bones and her grey hair was hidden under a brown headscarf. The door creaked open and then banged shut and Letty looked around the partition, seeing the coast was clear. She nodded at Suzy.

Suzy gripped the alarm in her palm and slunk into the old woman's room, which was bare except the straw on the floor, a blanket and pillow, and a bag with her clothes folded neat. Suzy put the alarm near the pillow under a heap of straw and returned.

"We'll see how she likes that racket." They had a good laugh thinking about her discovering it. At supper they sat at the Orthodox table picking at the potatoes and waiting for the lights in the barrack to shut off. Little was said, but their eyes caught each other bringing slight cracks of anticipation to their lips with each second that ticked.

When the lights snapped off across the camp for the night whispers were shushed by others. "Quiet, we are trying to sleep," or "Shhhhh!" or "I can hear your whispers, please quiet," rose through the barrack.

"There they go again, ruining the sleep of others," Mrs. Karpiniski said, now the unofficial Sheriff of Silence. "What's that ticking?" She said under her breath. Letty looked at Suzy in the dark, seeing the glow of her teeth, smiling and suppressing giggles. The Schmidt girls were the most quiet of the refugees that night.

The night's cold, gentle touch swept over the barrack as the rustles and voices transformed into rhythms of deep breathing. They waited, but soon succumbed to their subconscious. Dreams of beef shanks turned to Theo climbing a black mountain turned to mother scolding her for losing her shoes in Switzerland, "It was Annie, not me," Letty tried to tell her, but she started ringing bells with her hands "to drown out your lies."

Letty's eyes popped open and the ringing continued, as did her confusion about where she was. It kept ringing.

"Shut it off!"

"Who's making that racket?"

"Turn it off!"

"Someone's alarm is going off!"

The old woman was rolling around. "Oh dear, oh dear, oh dear," she said in a panicked fright.

"It's Mrs. Karpinski!" Suzy yelled, telling the entire barrack who was the culprit.

"Turn it off, Mrs. Karpinski!" Letty said. Then others in the barrack yelled at her to turn it off.

"You've woken everyone up, Mrs. Karpinski!" one woman said.

"It's not mine!" Mrs. Karpinski said. "Oh dear, here it is!" They heard the thuds of her bashing it against the floor to turn off its ringing.

"Please, Mrs. Karpinski!" others yelled. At last Mrs. Karpinski shut it off with a loud bang.

"It's not asking much for a peaceful sleep," Suzy said. "Thank you for shutting it off, Mrs. Karpinski."

"It's not mine," she said. "It's not."

"It came from your room!"

They started giggling in the dark and others laughed too.

"Shhhhhh. Please," voices said throughout the barrack. "Let us sleep!" And that was it. Mother's alarm clock came to a beautiful end.

60

Fear blinds you from the obvious.

A week went by and Rabbi Tauber brought more stacks of blankets. Their eyes asked the question their words did not. He shook his head in a short, fast burst that looked like a small seizure. He received no letters for them. The mail wasn't going through traditional routes and was inspected by the Vichy. The rabbi took armfuls of correspondence and mailed and received the letters for the refugees each visit.

The second week the rabbi handed out clothes with his wife. He stopped and sifted through the clothes handing Suzy a sweater, and in the sleeve was a letter. She opened it tearing at the sealed edge with her index finger. It was from mother and written in Polish. She was okay and spending time with her friends and was happy to stay in Lourdes. The idea of a smuggler didn't sit well with her. "I can't trust them," she said.

Annie grabbed a pen and scribbled out a letter trying to finish it before the rabbi left. "Dear Mother, You can make it. We know the smugglers. We know the route. We are safe and in good condition." Suzy found the rabbi before he walked out the door slipping him the letter. He stuffed it in his trench coat and put on his furry hat before stepping into the frigid evening.

The next week mother wrote again. She insisted on staying with her friends. "They look after me well." There were only so many ways to write and beg her to join them in Switzerland. Part of Letty wanted

251

to believe she sacrificed herself for her daughters to make it out of France. Part of her believed she didn't trust them enough to make the journey. And part of her believed she was too scared to do anything and so placed her fate in the hands of strangers, abandoning her own daughters.

61

Laugh at the absurdity, but enjoy it too.

Lausanne, Switzerland

In March of 1943 the captain announced women under 30 were being moved from Adliswil to another camp. They packed the clothes Rabbi Tauber gave them and along with 120 other women boarded trucks to an unknown destination. The military trucks spewed exhaust and grinded out of the barbed wire fenced camp.

The trucks thundered through the cozy town of Lausanne sitting on Lac Leman, which was surrounded by white-capped peaks. Southwest the trucks grumbled near Geneva. It was a bizarre mirage when they pulled up to a big iron gate that read "Villa Mont Choisi" ("Chosen Mountain House"), and even more bizarre when it drove through dropping them at an ivy-covered villa with balconies.

Their room's balcony overlooked a courtyard and there was a tennis court. A coffee shop in town had puff pastries that flaked and melted in their mouth. In the late afternoons they sunbathed on the balcony. It was like being at a fancy summer camp. They wrote and received letters from mother using a mailbox in town. They even caused trouble by taking off their stockings and dangling bare legs over the balcony in the spring sun. It was scandalous and prompted a loud knock on their door.

"I've received complaints," a policeman said when they opened their door. "Wives of men do not appreciate nudity. Proper young ladies should not be removing articles of clothing in a public setting."

"Oh, goodness," Suzy said. "We thought we were out of sight. We are so sorry!"

"Keep in mind people can see you on your balcony."

"Yes, or course officer." Satisfied, he tipped his cap and left.

"How dare you remove your stockings!" Suzy said in a deep voice. Their laughter was so loud the policeman now in the courtyard looked up at the room as he left the villa. They ducked their heads behind the ivy growing on the railing.

The spring breeze turned to summer heat and they wrote mother about learning to play tennis and the beautiful views of Lake Geneva, failing to mention their nude legs causing a ruckus with the married women. And so it went like summer camp until they were moved again.

62

The painful price for being right doesn't make you wrong.

Champery, Switzerland

As summer ended Swiss authorities relocated them to another town, Champery, a ski resort in the mountains. The views were stunning, but food was scarce. Letty was sent to work in the laundry room where she scrubbed the hotel's dirty linens. They wrote mother letting her know where they were sent, but mother's letters stopped coming. Letty inquired about the mail system and they double-checked their address and postage.

Letty's days were dictated by work and the search for food, and that was fine with her. It was her routine. Get up. Go to the laundry room. Get food rations. Check the mail and newspapers for morsels of information. Repeat. When new refugees came they brought news of the war and camps. She listened to their stories as she threw sheets into the tubs of hot water.

One day Letty was carrying a heap of sheets down the stairs and out of the corner of her eye she saw two people arriving with the fresh group of refugees. It's strange how peripheral vision can trigger recollection, but she dropped the dirty clothes in a pile and went near the two people, standing just far enough away for it not seem obvious she was snooping. Letty didn't know how she knew them, but had to figure it out. Her ears perked up and she listened to them talk and remembered the man's high-pitch voice. He wore a hat. She realized it was mother's friends from Lourdes. It was the man mother thought was so smart. They looked different. He had facial hair and she had her hair hidden under a scarf.

"Is it you, Elijah?" Letty said. He looked at her trying to place her face. "I'm Letty. My mother is Blima Schmidt."

"Oh, yes!" he said taking his hat off. "My dear, Letty. I heard you made it to Switzerland!"

"Is there any news of my mother? Her letters have stopped." He looked stunned and butterflies formed in Letty's stomach. They stood in the lobby of the Hotel Floret and stared at each other. He was searching for words.

"She went to Nice with my parents thinking it was safe there. The Italians were protecting Jews from the Vichy and Germans. We were told the Italians were going to evacuate 30,000 Jews to Italy. But in September the Italians and Allies struck a deal. The Nazis and Vichy pounced on Nice to tighten their hold. The Germans moved in before anyone was able to get out. They've been hunting Jews in the city and across France ever since. Your mother was caught in a *razzia* and sent to Drancy."

The air was taken from Letty's throat. Her jaw flexed wanting to say something, but there was nothing. Her green eyes glazed over and her vision retreated into her head and thoughts. The people mother thought would look after her were standing in front of Letty in the one place she said was a ridiculous idea, and refused to go to, Switzerland. It was a painful price, for being right.

63

Choose your heroes wisely.

Palo Alto, CA

It was too late; grandma was already dead and cremated. In a strange way, she passed much like her mother. Perhaps it was guilt, or a way to honor her mother, or just her subconscious playing out. Grandma had refused to move-in with her remaining daughter, didn't want anyone to come say goodbye, and that was that. I was told not to fly out and there was no memorial service. She disappeared with as little fanfare as possible and I lost my most important bridge to my mom with not even a bye. It felt as if I was seven again.

I remembered back to the pen marks all over my small fingers, and the dirt under my nails. Grandma had just finished telling me her story right after my mom died. "I drew you a picture," I said to her, pushing the pens out of the way and handing it to her.

In the wild array of colors and zigzag of lines and shapes, there were three figures running through the woods. There was a mountain in the background and a flag on top with a Nazi swastika. The woman in front had a big brown mop of hair and pointed her hand forward. It was the best I could draw at seven.

"Who is that?" grandma said.

"That's you." I searched my grandma's face for signs she understood the picture.

"Me? Okay, I see the resemblance. Tell me what's going on." Grandma sipped her tea.

"You're escaping the Nazis," I said. She studied it.

"That's a good picture. Are you sure you're seven-years-old?"

"You're saving them."

"I'm saving them?"

"Yes, you saved your family. You're a hero."

"You're too kind," she said and shook her head not accepting the compliment. Even so, in that moment as a boy, I knew if grandma survived, so could I. It was as if her story provided a roadmap for my own survival. She became my hero.

In her nest of artifacts and world treasures hanging from the walls was a picture. Grandma picked the photo up off the shelf. "This is my mother," she said. I'd seen it before, but never paid it any attention. Her mom had eyes that scorched the pleasantness out of life. Her wavy hair looked just like grandma's and they shared the same face.

"This was a print of the photo we tried to use for her fake papers. But it wasn't to be."

"What happened to her?" I asked.

"The French sent her in a boxcar to the Nazis." Grandma opened a drawer in the kitchen and found a computer print out. It was a list of names and she set it down on the table. "One thing you can say about the Nazis, they kept meticulous records. See here, this is their list of people they sent to the gas chambers at Auschwitz. That was my mother." She pointed to a name on the list.

"Blima Schmidt."

"They killed her?"

"Yes. And there's the date and convoy number."

BLIMA SCHMIDT

Date of Birth:	19 Mar 1891
Place of Birth:	BOJABOW
Convoy Number:	64
Date of Convoy:	7 Dec 1943
Convoy Destination:	AUSCHWITZ

U.S. Holocaust museum website, www.ushmm.org, screenshot by author.

Bundesarchiv, Bild 1011-027-1476-20A
Foto: Vennemann, Wolfgang | 24. Januar 1943

Jews being deported by train from southern France, 1943.

She left the paper on the table and lifted the picture of her mother and rubbed the dust off the edges and set it back on the shelf.

"She was not a nice woman, but she was my mother." Grandma sat down next to me.

"The war's end came too late for her. People celebrated in the streets when it was over. I sat there on the steps of the beautiful chalet in Switzerland wondering about my parents and my family." Grandma chuckled to herself and then fell silent for a moment. "200 members of my family wiped away: cousins including Bernard, uncles, aunts. All gone for no reason except religion."

She looked at the list and slid her index finger over the names. "That's my biggest regret in life. Not getting her out of France. She would've come if I had got her one. Would we have survived if she did? I don't know. We never even used the fake papers. Not once. But it gave us confidence."

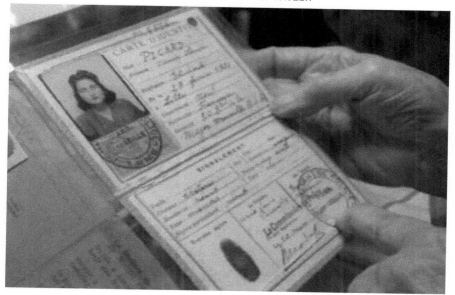

I looked at her face and saw the pain in the wrinkles around her eyes. After staring at the list grandma lifted her eyes to me. Her fingers clenched a tissue and she dabbed the corner of her lips, which trickled with saliva. In her mind she had either failed or abandoned her mother.

"For years I didn't let your mother play with German children," grandma said. "I remember one little boy your mother liked to play with at school. A nice, blonde boy, named Thomas.

"I walked to the school to get her each day. 'How was school, *bubala?*' I asked. Your mom was about your age and so smart. 'Good,' she said. 'That's my friend, Thomas.' She pointed to the boy and waved. He smiled and waved back.

"One day after school his parents came over to say hello and see about arranging a play date. They had thick accents and I asked where they were from. 'Germany,' they said. I felt uncontrollable anger shoot through my veins. I told them it was impossible and turned abruptly, leaving them standing with outstretched hands.

"I forbade your mom from playing with Thomas at school, or any other German. She screamed at me. I said, 'The decision is final!'

My voice pierced just like my mother's. I sometimes think about how confused that little boy must have been when your mom said she wasn't able to play with him anymore. It was a terrible thing to make your mom do. They were both blameless.

"The war has affected my decisions in ways I never expected, *boychick*. I carry that with me. And they affected your mom too." She shook her head and grimaced at the memory, and her guilt. Her eyes watered as they rested on me and she dabbed the creases around her mouth. I wondered if grandma was anything like her mother.

"Your mom loved you more than anything, Aaron. She fought so hard. I want you to know that. She wanted to live. To see you. It was just too much. She couldn't go on. But more than anything, she wanted to be with you."

64

Sometimes you win by losing.

Pittsburgh, PA

I still examine the floor of hospitals, conscious not to step on the cracks. This one today is wood laminate, not the white linoleum squares I remember as a child. Pictures of doctors hang on walls all the way down the corridor.

Now a world away from Afghanistan and American, Jew, spies and decades away from my grandma's experiences with the war. Yet, this day is just as dramatic and I lug heavy bags on my shoulders through the sterile halls. My grandma and mother aren't here to see this great day, but they are with me.

I now know why Grandma was so adamant about honoring my mother's last wishes in the hospital. When grandma eventually lost the court appeal to sell my house when I was a kid, I also know why she said, "Aaron, sometimes it's good to lose." In the months before her death she even told me, "Your father did a good job with you."

My mother's tree, planted by my grandma and her friends, is one of my mom's last vestiges. It is in a small, bucolic park with a Koi pond and gazebo near the white, cottage where I lived with her. As a child, and later as a teen, I walked from my house through the neighborhood streets to talk to her at the Gingko tree. I watched it grow from a sapling to a full tree with bright green leaves that turn gold in the fall.

It has a little plaque with her name and became the gravestone I always wanted as a child. I still pull leaves from the tree and press them inside the frame of her picture that hangs on the wall at our house.

I adjust the bags on my shoulder to open the door of the hospital room and set them down on those floors trying not to make a peep. I unzip one of the bags and take out a miniature stocking cap and a doll-sized shirt among the blankets and other clothes.

My beautiful wife, Beth, is propped up on a pillow holding our new baby girl. Beth's dark blonde hair is pushed back behind her ears, except for two stray curls. She is exhausted, but glowing with pure joy. My mom has a granddaughter, and my grandma has a great-granddaughter. A euphoric peace fills my chest and I can feel my smile at my ears.

I walk over and lift our baby up, cradling her fragile head in the crook of my arm. In time, I will tell her grandma's story, and my mother's. She yawns and I smell her sweet baby breath as it blows on my cheek. Her puffy eyes open and stare at me, studying my face. I kiss her on the forehead. "You're my little *bubala*. My sweet girl."

Epilogue

After the War

At the end of World War II, Letty and her sisters bounced around refugee camps in Switzerland. Letty was sent to *Schlosshilfikon*, "Punishment Camp," for dancing with a boy and remained there until the end of the war. Despite the severe name, the camp was nothing short of a gorgeous castle on a hill. During her stay she was introduced to poetry, classical music and was even allowed to invite boys to the castle. Letty forged a train ticket to the Netherlands and she found herself sitting in the British Officers car where she met Peter Bird, her future husband. He put his finger to his lips, "Your secret is safe with me." It wasn't until years later that Letty learned Theo did not survive the war when by a chance encounter she saw Daniel, Theo's friend from Luchon, at a bookstore in Toronto.

Annie married Shlomo (Stan) Lichtman, while in a camp in Tschiertschen. After the war they were among the first to be granted passage on a cruise ship to Palestine and joined cousin Hanka in Tel Aviv. Not long after, war broke out between the Jews and Arabs. Annie was forced to crawl with her infant son from her house, bullets whizzing over their heads, to escape. Along with two sons, Danny and Raffy, Annie and her husband joined Letty in Montreal, Canada, where Letty had settled with Peter.

Years later, Letty, Peter and two daughters, Karin and Kristina, moved from Montreal to California in search of work. Peter took a job as a civilian engineer with NASA.

Suzy married Paul Schweitzer, a non-Jewish man whom she met

in Switzerland. They settled in Basel and had two children, David and Fleur. While Letty forgave Suzy and visited her in Switzerland on numerous occasions, Annie and Suzy rarely spoke.

Many years after the war it was Suzy who met a woman in Basel that had access to records kept by the Nazis on the convoys of Jewish prisoners sent to Germany. She appealed for the information, and the woman sent her copies of documents, including one page detailing a train convoy from the camp in Drancy, France to Auschwitz. On the list of prisoners was their mother's name. It was the first time, decades after the war, the sisters had confirmation about the fate of their mother, Blima. Letty kept that list in her kitchen drawer. They never found out what happened to their father, Aron.

Suzy, Letty, Annie

Bibliography

Cesarani, David. *The Final Solution: Origins and Implementation*, Routledge, 1994.

Judge, Thomas, *Letty and Annie's Story*, 2006.

Lichtman, Annie. Video interview. Shoah Foundation, 2 July, 1997.

Marrus, Michael, and Paxton, Robert O., *Vichy France and the Jews*, Stanford University Press, 1995.

Obermaier, Ernst, *Die Ritterkreuztrager der Luftwaffe 1939-1945*, *Band I*, Verlag Dieter Hoffmann, Mainz, 1989.

Paldiel, Mordecai. *Churches and the Holocaust: Unholy Teaching, Good Samaritans, and Reconciliation*. Jersey City, NJ: KTAV, 2006.

Rajsfus, Maurice, *La Police de Vichy. Les Forces de l'ordre françaises au service de la Gestapo, 1940/1944*, Le Cherche-midi éditeur, 1995.

Warner, Geoffrey, *Pierre Laval and the Eclipse of France*, New York: The Macmillan Company, 1968.

Independent Commission of Experts, Switzerland – Second World War, *Switzerland and Refugees in the Nazi Era*, 1999.

Photo Credits

All photos and images are courtesy of Letty Bird's family except the following:

P. 74, courtesy of Bundesarchiv, Bild, *Philippe Pétain meeting Hitler in October 1940*, 183-H25217, CC-BY-SA 3.0 de (https://creativecommons.org/licenses/by-sa/3.0/de/legalcode).

P. 275, courtesy of Bundesarchiv, Bild, *French Jews being deported from Marseilles, 1943*, 101I-027-1476-20A, Vennemann, Wolfgang, CC-BY-SA 3.0 de (https://creativecommons.org/licenses/by-sa/3.0/de/legalcode).

About the Author

Aaron Rockett is a writer and video journalist. He has worked on numerous projects in Afghanistan including, *Inside the Taliban*, broadcast on the National Geographic Channel. Aaron holds a master's degree in strategic communication from American University and an undergraduate degree from Saint Mary's College of California.

You can connect with me on:
🌐 https://www.aaronrockett.com
🐦 https://twitter.com/Rockett_Books
📘 https://www.facebook.com/AaronRockettBooks

CPSIA information can be obtained
at www.ICGtesting.com
Printed in the USA
FFHW021849210319
51156185-56650FF